Praise for *Southern Life, Northern City*

"This book has an important place in articulating an aspect of African American history and culture poorly known and understood to date in American society and history."
— Gayle Graham Yates, author of
Life and Death in a Small Southern Town:
Memories of Shubuta, Mississippi

"Today, a national historic site, the Rapp Road community is a result of the endless and dedicated efforts of a daughter of that community, Emma Dickson, who brought much to bear to ensure that Rapp Road became a viable thread among many that went into 'the tapestry of Albany County.'"
— A. J. Williams-Myers,
State University of New York at New Paltz

"A fine local community study that invigorates our understanding and knowledge of the Great Migration of African Americans from south to north."
— Graham Russell Gao Hodges, Colgate University

Southern Life, Northern City

Southern Life, Northern City

The History of Albany's Rapp Road Community

JENNIFER A. LEMAK

excelsior editions
State University of New York Press
Albany, New York

Published by
STATE UNIVERSITY OF NEW YORK PRESS, ALBANY

For information, contact State University of New York Press, Albany, NY
www.sunypress.edu

Production by Diane Ganeles
Marketing by Susan M. Petrie

Excelsior Editions is an imprint of State University of New York Press

Library of Congress Cataloging-in-Publication Data

Lemak, Jennifer A.
  Southern life, northern city : the history of Albany's Rapp Road
Community / Jennifer A. Lemak.
      p. cm.
  Includes bibliographical references and index.
  ISBN 978-0-7914-7581-2 (hc : alk. paper) 978-0-7914-7582-9 (pb : alk. paper)
    1. African Americans—New York (State)—Albany—History. 2. African
Americans—New York (State)—Albany—Interviews. 3. Rapp Road
Community (Albany, N.Y.)—History. 4. Rapp Road Community (Albany,
N.Y.)—Social life and customs. 5. Community life—New York (State)—
Albany—History. 6. African American neighborhoods—New York (State)—
Albany—History. 7. Albany (N.Y.)—History. 8. Albany (N.Y.)—Social life
and customs. 9. African Americans—Migrations—History. 10. Migration,
Internal—United States—History. I. Title.

F129.A39N4 2008
974.7'43—dc22   2008000257

10 9 8 7 6 5 4 3 2 1

To Emma Dickson, for being a historian at heart

Contents

Illustrations

Preface

I first became aware of the Rapp Road community in 2000 when I enrolled in a graduate seminar in local and regional history at the University at Albany. Each student was asked to find a different aspect of Albany's history and write a twenty-five page research paper. After listening to other students' topics and still not having one of my own, the instructor asked if anyone would do a paper on African American history in Albany; I volunteered. At the time, I was employed at the Albany Institute of History and Art and decided to talk with the Curator of History, Wesley Balla, for some ideas on possible African American research projects. Balla came back with a list of ideas that spanned the eighteenth through the twentieth centuries. The very last one he mentioned, which he said could be very interesting but potentially difficult to research, was the Rapp Road community. Balla had visited Rapp Road and had spoken with community leader and resident Emma Dickson, because she was hoping to have the community placed on the New York State Historic Register in an effort to slow down commercial development that threatened her community.

Balla shared his initial research regarding the community and invited me to a lecture on the history of Rapp Road given by Emma Dickson. I attended the lecture, where Dickson showed family photographs and told stories about growing up on Rapp Road. Several family and church members were in the audience who told stories as well. I remember sitting in the auditorium during the presentation thinking "How on earth could a group of people from Shubuta, Mississippi, end up in Albany, New York?" The stories I heard that night were so dramatic and interesting that I knew then that I wanted to research the Rapp Road community.

I contacted John J. McEneny, New York State Assemblyman and local historian, who put me in contact with former Rapp Road resident and the New York State Assembly's Sergeant at Arms, Wayne Jackson. Jackson in turn gave me Dickson's phone number. I called Dickson and told her I wanted to write a research paper on the history of her community. She invited me to her home on Rapp Road and we spoke about the project at length. Dickson told me that she wanted the community placed on the New York State Historic Register in an effort to stop the Pyramid Crossgates Corporation from infringing on the community more than it already had. I told her my research paper could serve as the basis of the historic registry nomination, but I would have to conduct oral history interviews with community members in order to gather information. Dickson knew that an outsider of the community, whether white or black, could not just show up at residents' homes and ask for information. Dickson arranged for all of my initial interviews. Her oldest sister, two cousins, two first-generation Rapp Road residents, and one of the church mothers were my first interviewees. These interviews served as the basis of my research paper.

After that semester, I still found the history of the community fascinating and felt there was still much more to research. I told Dickson that I would write the nomination for the historic registry. We both worked with John Bonafide, Historic Preservation Services Coordinator at the New York State Office of Parks, Recreation, and Historic Preservation. He told us what information he needed for the nomination process and we either gathered the information together, or I gathered it and reported my findings. As this process continued, Dickson and I became friends, and I think she enjoyed that I took a genuine interest in her family's stories and community's history. Anytime I went to visit her, she would tell me multiple stories about her family. She also pestered fellow community members to tell their stories and insisted that they give me old photographs.

As word about the Rapp Road history project spread around the Capital District, Dickson and I began giving lectures. Rapp Road history became popular with local history organizations, particularly during Black History Month. I discussed the history of the Great Migration, and Dickson told stories about her family and the community.

During this time, I decided to expand my Rapp Road research and make it the basis for my doctoral dissertation. Dickson was genuinely excited by this. In November 2002, Dickson and her oldest sister, Girlie Ferguson, and I spent five days in Shubuta, Mississippi, conducting interviews with family members and others associated with Albany or the Rapp Road community. Our research trip to Mississippi was a complete success. Many of the stories we heard from migrants in Albany about how hard life was in Mississippi were validated by stories from those who stayed behind in Shubuta.

As my dissertation research continued, my relationship with the Rapp Road residents grew. In September 2002, I sat with Dickson and other Rapp Road residents—all of us anxiously waiting—at the New York State Historic Preservation Board meeting while the community's proposal was reviewed and voted on. When the nomination passed, I was just as excited as the community's residents. The designation of Rapp Road as a New York State Historic District encouraged the residents to take a new pride in their community and family histories. One of my proudest moments came the following summer during the annual Rapp Road family reunion weekend when the community not only celebrated the historic designations, but also honored Dickson and me at a black-tie reception and dinner.

My dissertation was completed in 2004, but my research and relationship with the community continued as Rapp Road became the subject of two museum exhibitions, countless public lectures, walking tours, and the impetus for the establishment of the Rapp Road Historical Association. If anything of historical significance was going on in the community, I usually received a call and happily participated. After I found out I was pregnant with my first child, one of my initial calls was to Dickson to see if there was room at her day care on Rapp Road. As it turns out, I am on Rapp Road everyday to pick up my daughter. On many days, Dickson and I have a quick Rapp Road history–centered conversation before I get the report on my child. Our research continues as we try to piece together the past. Even in 2007, as I was preparing the manuscript for this book, residents relayed new stories and old photographs were still being brought out of albums and boxes.

This study would not have been possible without the support of the entire Rapp Road community and most of all Emma Dickson who supported this research from the beginning. She shared the information she had been collecting for over two decades. It is because of Emma Dickson that I was able to conduct oral history interviews with community and church members. My two research trips to Mississippi would not have been possible without the support of a University at Albany Initiatives for Women Research Grant and a University at Albany Office of Research Benevolent Grant. During these trips to Mississippi, much information was collected because of the help of Girlie Ferguson, Emma Dickson, Alonzo McCann, Jerry Mason, James Sheehe, Jr., Brian Buff, and the staff at the Mississippi Department of Archives and History.

In addition, I would like to thank Dr. Ivan Steen, Director of the University at Albany Public History Program, and Stefan Bielinski, Senior Historian at the New York State Museum, two first-rate historians, who helped me through this entire process. I am also thankful for the support of the New York State Museum for both the Doctoral Research Fellowship Program and my current employment as Senior Historian, to Dr. John Hart, Director of Research and Collections, and the entire history staff at the New York State Museum. I extend my gratitude to historian Wesley Balla for introducing me to the Rapp Road community and sharing his initial research and valuable historical insights and to John Bonafide, New York State Historic Preservation Services Coordinator, for his perseverance with the Rapp Road Historic District nomination.

Lastly, I am grateful to my family: to my parents Janeen and James Sheehe and Joseph Lemak, Jr., for the love, education, and encouragement imparted to me, and to my husband, Brian, and children, India and Duncan, whom I love very much.

Introduction

In January 2003, the Rapp Road community was added to the list of National Historic Districts. This little-known African American community located in the western extension of Albany, New York, is a distinctive product of the Great Migration. The Rapp Road community is an example of a rural chain migration community that was established in the early 1930s and continues to thrive today. Each of the remaining thirteen families currently living or owning property on Rapp Road can be traced back to the rural South, with the majority of them to Shubuta, Mississippi.

The Rapp Road community is the result of a vision by Louis W. Parson. Parson and his wife, Frances, migrated to Albany from Shubuta around 1927. A traveling preacher in Mississippi, Parson decided to start his own church in Albany, The First Church of God in Christ. To increase church membership Parson traveled back and forth between Mississippi and Albany personally relocating many African Americans. Word of mouth about Albany spread, and families from Shubuta moved north without waiting for Parson to bring them.

Most of the families migrating from Mississippi moved to Albany's South End where the majority of African Americans lived at this time. During the first half of the twentieth century the South End was the center of Albany's gambling, drinking, and prostitution. As a result, these deeply religious southern migrants did not want to raise their families in this environment. Realizing that members of his congregation were unhappy living in the South End, Louis

1

Parson set out to remedy the situation. On 2 May 1930, Elder Parson and church member William Toliver purchased a fourteen-acre tract of land. Three years later Parson and his wife purchased a second fourteen-acre tract of land. Both tracts were located in the western extension of the city of Albany known as the Pine Bush. The area Parson purchased was rural, surrounded only by a few farms, and looked similar to Shubuta. Elder Parson's plan was to sell tracts of land to his congregation so they could get away from city life.

Parson's plan was successful, resulting in the community that is still vibrant today. Rapp Road residents built homes, planted gardens, hunted, raised families, and essentially recreated their rural southern life. Ties between Shubuta and Albany remain strong as friends and family travel back and forth for the biannual Shubuta homecoming and the annual Rapp Road reunion.

FACTORS LEADING TO THE GREAT MIGRATION

The Rapp Road community is a result of the Great Migration, a period between 1910 and 1940 of rapid population shift when hundreds of thousands of southern African Americans resettled in the North hoping to find better employment, housing, education for their children, and less racial discrimination. However, upon arrival in the North, blacks found hard, dirty, industrial employment, poor housing, mediocre schools, and racial discrimination. Yet, African Americans continued to flock to the North's urban centers until the 1960s. A look at the economic, cultural, and political factors in the South that contributed to the Great Migration gives insight into why southern African Americans in general and the original Rapp Road residents in particular traveled to the North despite its harsh realities.

The political schema in the South prior to World War I had not changed much since post–Civil War Reconstruction. Jim Crow laws, like the black codes and the slave codes, were legally mandated laws designed to replace the social controls of slavery and thus insured racial segregation between 1877 and the 1950s. These laws maintained that blacks and whites were not social equals. Blacks suffered with inferior schools, libraries, hospitals, law enforcement, and public accommodations. To make matters worse, blacks were not recognized by the judicial system. If they were found guilty of a petty crime, they could be put into a chain gang and forced to work. Dogs and guns hunted down black sharecroppers who left their plantation before their debt was paid or the harvest gathered.[1] In his book about the Great Migration, Peter Gottlieb stated, "The real slavery of buying and selling blacks before the Civil War gave way to the semi-slavery of peonage, convict lease labor, and the exchanging of black tenants' debts among white landowners."[2]

Furthermore, blacks had few options at the voting polls. Many blacks did not vote because they had to pass difficult literacy tests, pay a large poll tax, own property, or were threatened with violence. Worse than these intimidations, many felt that their vote would not make any difference. Eddie McDonald, an African American migrant from Mississippi, said that he "remembers having to look at a jar of jelly beans and be able to know how many there were before they would let blacks vote."[3] Not having a voice in government was one of the reasons McDonald migrated to Chicago, Illinois. Disenfranchised southern African Americans had no political recourse to change the politics and laws that kept them poverty-stricken. As a result, many looked to the North as a political and economic arena they could participate in and benefit from. Upon arrival in the North, many new migrants immediately registered to vote. In some instances the large number of blacks voting as a block swayed an election for a candidate. For example, in Chicago's 1915 mayoral election, William Hale Thompson won because the majority of African Americans voted for him.[4]

Cultural factors in the South best illustrate why such a large number of African Americans moved north. Blacks were considered and treated like second-class citizens in the South. Segregation and oppression were widespread, and southern society would not allow African Americans to succeed. Working hard as an employee was unlikely to bring advancement. Historian James Grossman found that "most black southerners were well aware of the 'Dixie limit' beyond which no black could advance."[5] Signs of black prosperity could attract white retaliation and violence.

White southerners created a culture of fear for African Americans. When laws were violated, blacks faced injustice before the law. For example, the Mississippi Pig Law passed in 1876 declared that theft of a pig, swine, or property over ten dollars by an African American was punishable by up to five years in jail.[6] This extreme law resulted in overcrowding of Mississippi prisons, mainly by African Americans. Furthermore, because of Jim Crow laws, blacks were not allowed to sit on juries. Biased juries freed guilty whites and sent innocent blacks to jail. Most of all, southern blacks lived in an overall hostile social environment, which included lynching as a form of punishment. Lynching was used against blacks as a form of intimidation. Southern blacks, both men and women, were lynched for owning property, voting, testifying in court against a white person, and failing to express deference to whites. Between 1882 and 1962, Mississippi had 538 black lynchings (the highest number in the United States), Georgia had 491, Texas had 352, Louisiana had 335, Alabama had 299, and Tennessee had 204.[7] The total number of known black lynchings in the United States between 1882 and 1962 was 3,442.[8]

In addition to the southern culture of fear, there was a culture of control over blacks. This sense of control was defined the most by Jim Crow laws and the system of sharecropping. Jim Crow laws, similar to the nineteenth-century Black Codes, controlled where southern blacks were allowed to go and what they were allowed to do. The majority of black southerners during this time were sharecropping farmers. This form of employment controlled several aspects of one's life. Sharecroppers rented plots of land, housing, seeds, and equipment and bought on credit food and clothing, if needed, from the plantation owner. Thus, the plantation owners had control over the tenant's life. The sharecropper repaid the plantation owner with a portion of his crop returns. Many times the sharecropper's debts were so high the owner received the majority of the harvest and the sharecropper was stuck renting from the owner for another year. This cycle of indebtedness could limit the options of black farmers for long periods of time.[9] Those farmers who were lucky enough to stay out of debt and break even with their harvest still faced dishonest plantation owners who could "cook the books."[10]

Sharecropping contracts in the South were enforced by criminal laws instead of civil laws that formed a legal system that dramatically strengthened the owner's control.[11] If a renter decided to leave a plantation before the end of his contract, the owner could file a criminal suit against him. Criminal suits often resulted in harsh punishments. Often debt-ridden sharecroppers who wanted to migrate north had to sneak off their plantations.

Southern blacks associated freedom and racial equality with the North long before the Great Migration. Slavery was not as widespread in the North as it was in the South, and the North was the home of the abolitionist movement and equal rights activity throughout the nineteenth century. Some of the African Americans who migrated to northern cities at the end of the nineteenth century were better educated and more affluent than the black southern laborers who migrated en masse during and after World War I; as a result, many were successful in northern cities. Word of African American success traveled south. James Grossman states in his book on the Great Migration, "The most influential travelers were earlier migrants who returned home to visit, looking prosperous and urbane and bursting with wondrous tales of their exploits. Although most migrants used the mail to report their progress, many could not resist returning 'just to tell how well they had done in the North.' "[12]

The racial oppressiveness of the South made the North seem like the Promised Land to many rural black sharecroppers, who often left their homes in the middle of the night and started north.

Several economic factors contributed to the Great Migration. Before World War I began in 1914, few African Americans were economically prosperous. The majority of northern blacks were manual laborers, domestic servants, or both. In the South, most blacks were sharecropping farmers, manual laborers, and domestic servants. This changed with the start of World War I. The flow of European immigrants to the United States was halted. As a result, there were fewer immigrants to fill lower-level manufacturing jobs, so northern manufacturers dropped their racial biases and hired African Americans for the first time. It is estimated that 400,000 African Americans took manufacturing jobs in northern cities before the end of World War I.[13] In manufacturing centers like Pittsburgh and Chicago southern blacks were recruited as strikebreakers during labor disputes. Unfortunately, black strikebreakers were generally discharged after a labor strike.[14] Labor agents who traveled south to recruit blacks for work in northern factories were used as scapegoats by white southerners not willing to accept the underlying causes of the Great Migration.[15] According to Grossman, "In Mississippi, imprisonment and a $500 fine awaited any agent guilty of 'inducing' labor from the state."[16]

A second factor contributing to migration was that wages in the North were higher than the agriculturally based wages in the South. When word of this traveled south, many blacks made the decision to leave. A third economic factor contributing to the Great Migration was the series of economic setbacks prior to World War I that hit southern farmers hard. There, the boll weevil, an insect that attacks the cotton boll, ruined crops across the South beginning in 1903 when it hit Louisiana. The boll weevil continued eastward every few years. Mississippi suffered the most crop destruction. The boll weevil hit in 1907 and culminated its destruction in 1913. Alabama was hit after 1916.[17] Black southern farmers were continually forced to move away from the crop devastation. In addition, a series of major storms and floods occurred across the South, further ruining crops during this time.

All of this destruction resulted in poor crop returns for farmers. As a result, landowners tightened credit making it even more difficult for black sharecroppers to break even. When banks began to fold and loans became impossible to secure, farm owners were forced to sell their land at low prices. This put tenants in the even worse situation of limited advances of food and clothing, while increasing the already high interest rates they paid.[18]

The political, cultural, and economic situation in the South pushed many African Americans out. Simultaneously the situation in the North pulled discontented African Americans to move there. These push and pull factors resulted in the Great Migration.

Through oral history interviews this book will examine the relatively unknown story of a chain migration community during the Great Migration as interpreted by the migrants and their families. This study investigates the movement of southern blacks to Albany, New York. It records and documents the establishment of the Rapp Road community by tracing the migrants' journey from Shubuta, Mississippi, to the South End of Albany, New York, and finally to landownership on Rapp Road. Also, by using the process of community-based historical research, the Rapp Road community is studied from its inception to its imperiled future by commercial development, and lastly, to community preservation.

CHAPTER 1

Shubuta, Mississippi: Home of the Red Artesian Well

Migration fever hit Shubuta, Mississippi, and its surrounding areas in the beginning of the twentieth century and black families began traveling north to find a better life. In fact, so many blacks began leaving Shubuta that the local paper, *The Mississippi Messenger*, published the article, "Negroes Should Remain in South," on 5 September 1919.[1] The article stated that blacks were not treated poorly and good employment was available. "They [three black surveyors from Chicago] declare they can now recommend that Negroes come south to find work; they assert they found no basis for the northern allegations that Mississippi would bear such a libelous epithet; they investigated farm labor conditions near a dozen cities and at the Archman convict farms; they discovered that Negroes could walk on the sidewalks of Mississippi cities without being lynched. . . ."[2] Despite this article and these supposed adequate conditions, African Americans wanted to leave Shubuta because of poor employment opportunities, poor educational facilities, and discrimination. These migrants left home seeking a better life for themselves and their families. A large number of the black migrants who left the Shubuta area moved to Albany, New York, during the 1930s and 1940s when Louis W. Parson moved north in

9

1927 and began returning by car to drive Mississippi blacks north. News of Albany spread by word of mouth, and blacks also left the area by train and bus.

Shubuta, located on the Chickasawhay River, was established around 1833 after the area was ceded to the United States from the Choctaw Indians with the Treaty of the Dancing Rabbit Creek on 27 September 1830.[3] The word "Shubuta" is derived from the Choctaw Indian word *Shoboti*, meaning "smoky." The Indians applied this name to the creek that is an arm of the Chickasawhay River with smoke-colored waters.[4] Clarke County (the county in which Shubuta is located) was named after Judge Joshua C. Clarke, a native of Pennsylvania, a delegate to the Mississippi Constitutional Convention in 1817, and a Justice of the Mississippi Supreme Court.[5] Clarke County was established in 1833.[6]

In 1855, the Mobile and Ohio Railroad came through Shubuta, and with it came shops and a depot. With the railroad came an increased population and prosperity. Shubuta was incorporated on 8 November 1865. The railroad brought many businesses such as hotels, restaurants, druggists, dry goods stores, and a furniture store. In 1879 the town's first newspaper the *Mississippi Messenger*, was established and published by C. A. Stovall.[7] During the late nineteenth century, Shubuta was the biggest city between Meridian, Mississippi, and Mobile, Alabama. In 1890 Shubuta's population was 4,115 and in 1900 it was 4,316.[8] Beginning in the late 1920s and 1930s Shubuta's population began to slowly drop as the result of the closing of the Mobile and Ohio Railroad's shops in Shubuta and the destroyed agricultural economy because of the boll weevil infestation.[9]

FAMILY STRUCTURE

Shubuta's black population in 1930 was 2,359, which was 56.6 percent of the total population (4,170).[10] African American family structures in Shubuta were consistent with the rural South on the whole. Almost half (49.6 percent) of the 256 African American households in Shubuta in 1930 were considered nuclear.[11] In a study of the black family Herbert Gutman claimed, "The nuclear household retained its commanding importance among rural blacks . . . the typical southern black household in 1900 still had at its head a lower-class husband or father."[12] A nuclear family denotes two parents and children or a husband and wife. According to the census, 26.6 percent of the black households in Shubuta were classified as extended, meaning the nuclear family plus one or more relatives. Only 7.8 percent of African American households were classified as augmented, which is defined as a family unit plus one or more non-kin. Non-kin could be lodgers, boarders, servants, or apprentices. Lastly, 1.6 percent of households were extended and augmented; meaning both kin and non-kin lived with the family unit.[13] Gutman theorized that the existence of extended and augmented households in the South were adaptive strategies for dealing with the poverty that most blacks knew.[14] According to the order in which the census was taken, many families with the same last name lived next door to each other, or in close proximity. This phenomenon is also supported in the oral history interviews. Only 8.6 percent of African American households in Shubuta were one-parent families, and 5.5 percent were single-person households. In most cases, 90.9 percent, one-parent households were the result of death of the spouse. The majority, 81.6 percent, of Shubuta's households were male headed. This is also consistent with Gutman's study: "Most southern black women headed neither households nor subfamilies. Far greater numbers of unmarried black women under thirty, for example, lived with their parents than headed households."[15]

The largest group, 38.3 percent, of African American households in Shubuta were childless, while 33.2 percent of the households had one to two children, 8.9 percent of the households had three to four children, 11.0 percent of the households had five to six children, 6.2 percent of the households had seven to eight children, and lastly, 2.4 percent of the households had nine to ten children. No households had more than ten children.[16] Lastly, 50.4 percent of African American families owned their own home, while 41.0 percent rented.[17]

In 1937 the Works Progress Administration (WPA) historical research project reported the following on African American homes in Wayne County (located less than two miles from Shubuta). "The homes of the negroes are mostly small unscreened frame buildings. The sanitary conditions of most of these homes leave much to be desired. However there are a few well built and screen homes and many are kept as clean as conditions will permit."[18] Despite poor living and economic conditions for southern African American families prior to and during the Great Migration, African American families remained intact. Shubuta families were no different (see appendix 2).

BLACK CHURCHES IN SHUBUTA

For many African Americans in Shubuta, and the South in general, religion was a huge part of their lives. Church was a vehicle for African Americans to express themselves, form communities, and find refuge in the hostile South. E. Franklin Frazier, in his 1964 book about the history of the black church in America wrote: "The Negro church with its own forms of religious worship was a world which the white man did not invade but only regarded with an attitude of condescending amusement. . . . What mattered was the way he was treated in the church which gave him an opportunity for self-expression and status . . . he could always find an escape from such, often painful, experiences within the shelter of his church."[19] According to several oral history interviews, devotion to God and attending church were important aspects of black Shubuta residents' identity.

In the beginning of the twentieth century there was only one official black church in Shubuta, the First Baptist Church.[20] By 1936 there were several small black congregations in Shubuta and surrounding rural areas. Most black churches were small, one-room buildings. Country ministers often traveled to many congregations to preach on different days of the week, and as a result blacks attended services at several different churches. Many of these rural churches held services monthly and had between fifteen and two hundred parishioners. In an interview, Shubuta resident Willis McDonald talks about going to many churches. "I go to Center Ridge Baptist Church in DeSoto [Mississippi]...I go to more than that one. I go to her church [his wife's church, St. Matthew Baptist]. And then I go to Mt. Zion. I praise him everywhere. I don't have discrimination on any church. They are all serving for the same purposes. That's the way I feel."[21]

Table 1. Black Churches, Pastors, and Membership in Shubuta, Mississippi, 1936

Church	Pastor	Membership
Altare	S. D. Arrington, Heidelberg	65
Bethlehem	W. A. Hardaway	156
New Zion	E. Lands	30
Pleasant Grove	F. D. Bender	55
New Salem		
St. Mary	Fred Bender	85
St. Matthew Baptist		90
Tribulation	W. A. Hardaway	75
Moses Temple	W. A. Hardaway	
St. Paul		
Sweet Pilgrim		

Source: Eva Haney and Anna B. Hardee, "History of Clarke County Mississippi," Assignment #26 (Washington, D.C.: Federal Writers Project, 1936), 41–42.

Alma McDonald, born in Shubuta in 1928, remembers going to church when she was a child. "I went to that church right in town . . . St. Matthew Baptist Church. Grandma used to take me there. . . . I joined this church when I was seven years old. I was baptized in . . . well they did not have anything to baptize you in, so I was baptized in the creeks. So my grandmother took all of us to the creeks and the preacher and everybody and we were baptized in Shubuta Creek. That last creek you ran over coming into Shubuta on [Route] 45. A lot of people were baptized in that creek."[22] Because there was no church in their rural area, the Franklin family from Chicora, Mississippi, traveled weekly for church to what they considered to be the "city" of Shubuta.[23]

Interviews reveal that many blacks had strong faith in God and their churches, which enabled them to deal with the harsh realities of living in rural Mississippi in the first half of the twentieth century. Discrimination and racism did not stop at the church door, thus the need for blacks to establish their own churches. W. E. B. Du Bois explained this phenomenon in one of his speeches: "[I]f there was any fellowship between Christians, white and black, it would be after the manner explained by a white Mississippi Clergyman in all seriousness: 'The Whites and Negroes understand each other here perfectly, sir, perfectly; if they come to my church they take a seat in the gallery. If I go to theirs, they invite me to the front pew or the platform.' "[24] Many preachers equated the black oppression in the South with the oppression of the Jews in the Old Testament. Moses leading the Jews out of Egypt was equated with African Americans moving north away from their oppressors.[25] For many Shubuta residents who did not migrate, church and their faith gave them reasons to continue living in the South despite the oppression. This faith is what gave other Shubuta residents the hope for a better life in the North.

EDUCATION

According to the 1930 census only 22.3 percent of black children in Shubuta under the age of eighteen attended school.[26] Educational opportunities for African Americans in Shubuta, and the South in general, were limited. Public schools were segregated and funding for them was not equal to that of white schools.[27] A 1930 letter from Mississippi State Education Agent P. H. Easom states the salary schedule for a Mississippi summer high school teacher was $300 for director, $250 for a white instructor, $250 for a black principal, and $150 for a black instructor.[28] Many African American schools only ran for six months out of the year because children were expected to help their families with farm work.[29] According to the Public School Register of 1875, there were only two schools for black children in Clarke County, while there were thirty small schools for white children.[30] By 1936 there were about forty schools for black children.[31] "Most of them [the schools for black children] are small one-teacher schools scattered throughout the county but have the average equipment with the average efficiency for colored schools."[32] White children had larger, well-equipped, modern schools that included the Shubuta Institute and Military Academy and the Shubuta Female Academy.[33]

The schools for black children in Clarke County were inadequate enough for the Rosenwald Fund to erect two new schools in the 1920s, in Shubuta and Quitman, specifically for rural black children. Julius Rosenwald, the son of German Jewish immigrants, lived in Chicago and worked as an executive for the Sears Roebuck mail-order company. Around the turn of the century, Rosenwald believed the state of education for blacks in the South was horrible and wanted to help. In 1912 the wealthy philanthropist paired up with Booker T. Washington to create a challenge grant program that led to the construction of 4,977 rural schools for black children.[34] In Clarke County both of these schools were junior high schools. In 1936, the Rosenwald Junior High School, located in Shubuta, was valued at $2,500. The school's three rooms were partially equipped with patent desks, window shades, a small library, and a piano.[35] In a Federal Writers Project (FWP) interview the school's principal, Sam Adams, said: "There are four teachers and nine grades of work. Friday afternoon literary programs are given; regular meetings of Parent Teacher Association; and Faculty meetings are called. Baseball and basketball games are played."[36] This was a big improvement over the area's other black schools.

Girlie Ferguson, born in 1927, went to a segregated school in Hattiesburg, Mississippi, until the fourth grade. She recalled

> As far as I can remember, school was great. We had a regular, modern school, although the homemaking building was not directly connected to the school building. And we had regular flush toilets that were outside the school building. We had a regular classroom just like any other classroom. The fun part of going to school in Hattiesburg was the end of the year, which was in May, we always had these plays, and each class had a play and that was fun times because we got to be in these plays. I remember as a little girl, having a daisy costume made out of crepe paper.[37]

During school Ferguson lived with her grandparents because their house was closer than her parent's house to her school. She walked seven miles to school each way. The only thing Ferguson was afraid of while living with her grandparents was that if she played on her way to school, and was late, she would be punished.[38]

AFRICAN AMERICAN EMPLOYMENT

The biggest form of employment for African Americans in Shubuta was farming. According to the 1930 United States Census, there

were 485 farms with a total of 47,404 acres of land in Shubuta on
1 April 1930.[39] Less than half, 43 percent (110), of the 256 African
American families who resided in Shubuta in 1930 lived on a farm,
while 49 percent (118) of household heads in Shubuta were farmers
or farm laborers.[40]

According to Girlie Ferguson, whose parents and grandparents were sharecroppers in Shubuta, life during the early
twentieth century was hard for most blacks. Farming was a low-
paying, difficult occupation. Farmers worked long, labor-intensive
days in extreme heat and hoped for a good crop return. School-
aged children worked on farms to help their families. As a result,
black children attended school only six months out of the year in
Mississippi.[41] Furthermore, sharecroppers and tenant farmers often
had to deal with dishonest landlords. W. E. B. Du Bois agreed
that harsh treatment toward African American sharecroppers was
common. In his book *The Souls of Black Folk*, Du Bois noted: "Just
as centuries ago it was no easy thing for the serf to escape into the
freedom of town-life, even so today there are hindrances laid in
the way of county laborers. In considerable parts of all the Gulf
States, and especially in Mississippi, Louisiana, and Arkansas, the
Negroes on the plantations in the back-country districts are still
held at forced labor practically without wages."[42]

Sharecropping was a landlord-tenant relationship in which
the tenant cultivated the owner's land and received a percentage
of the profits, in either money or crops. Crops included cotton,
corn, sweet potatoes, watermelons, and black-eyed peas.[43] Often
the tenants had to buy or rent seeds, equipment, and animals
from the landowners. Vernon Lane Wharton discussed some of
the discriminations facing black sharecroppers in Mississippi in his
book *The Negro in Mississippi*. He wrote

These small merchants [owners of small stores], often operating
on credit themselves, wrote enormous mark-ups onto the prices
of the goods they sold to planters or Negroes for payment at

the end of the season. The mark-up in the Summit region in 1871 was 100 per cent, raising the price of meal to seventy-five cents per bushel, of fat meat to twenty-six cents per pound, and molasses to one dollar per gallon. . . . In cases where the planter bought the supplies on his own credit and passed them on to the Negroes, the price generally underwent another increase.[44]

Interviews indicate that not only did landowners try to cheat their black tenants out of money, but also out of crops. The result was that the sharecropper constantly owed money to the landowner. Sam McCann, a migrant from Mississippi, was the target of a dishonest landowner in Shubuta. Girlie Ferguson, one of McCann's several grandchildren, said her grandfather and parents bought products from the landowner's store using the credit he had from their wages. Although McCann and other family members knew exactly how much credit he was supposed to have, the landowner's wife allegedly changed the numbers in his account to make it look like he constantly owed money.[45] As a result, Ferguson said, the entire family—grandparents, parents, aunts, uncles, cousins, and siblings—decided to move to Hattiesburg, Mississippi, where two of her uncles were already working. Ferguson's father, Alfred Woodard, got a job working at Harper's Dairy Farm and Ferguson's grandfather, Sam McCann, got a job working on another farm.[46]

Fred Thomas, a longtime Shubuta resident spoke about his experience sharecrop farming between 1930 and 1932.

They [migrants moving from Shubuta to Albany] just counted on it was better time up there than it was here. It had been rough . . . I was working for four bits a day . . . fifty cents a day . . . working forking the field and with the plow. I also worked in the sawmill. . . . And the railroad laying track and ties, spike them down. . . . I didn't go north because I had a family. I was living out on Mag Stanley's [a large plantation owned by Maggie Stanley] . . . we were farming down there and we had never been nowhere, so we just stayed around. I think I left there [the

Stanley plantation] in [19]32. I was treated all right. . . . I would be there plowing with Miss Maggie and they wouldn't be able to buy me feed. We would plow mules in the day and turn them out at night. . . . It had been just so rough down here, just so rough. After I stayed there two years and didn't make no money, I left. At the end of the year I would never clear nothing out of my cotton crops. . . . I wouldn't owe her [Maggie Stanley] anything, but she came and got all my cotton and paid for what I had got. I ain't owing her when I left, not a thing in the world . . . After I got on my own I started making money.[47]

Geneva Conway, the daughter of sharecrop farmers in Shubuta, Mississippi, in the 1930s, recalls that farming was so difficult for her father that he had to move out of town to try and make a profit.

My dad was a sharecropper. He had a wife and three children. My mother's family had always owned land and held their own. So they were always respected in this very small community [Shubuta, Mississippi], which is like a wide place in the middle of the road. My dad was a sharecropper. When he got ready to move us out of that environment of always working and never having any money at the end of the year; you always owed at the end of the year. He wanted to take us to Mobile [Alabama] to his sister's. He had to leave at night. He had to walk fourteen miles at night; he couldn't even catch the bus where we lived. He had to go away to catch a bus. By the time the sharecropper realized my father was gone, my father was in Mobile.

Then my mother and her three little children had to live and go back to safety and security on my grandfather's property because the High Sheriff would not come up to Sam McCall's place and cause trouble [because he was well respected in the community.] But he [the Sheriff] would cause trouble in several other places. He came with a gun, I was a little girl with my mother, and he wanted to know where Wash [Conway's father] was. But because she was Sam McCall's daughter, he didn't bother her. Our parents suffered greatly for where we are today.[48]

Farming was such a physically intensive occupation that often children would help the family with chores. Eddie Johnson Burton, a migrant to Albany originally from Mathensville, Mississippi (approximately eight miles from Shubuta), grew up on the farm her father sharecropped. The family consisted of seven girls and three boys. "I never had to plow . . . my dad tried to teach me how to plow cotton, but I said I'm gonna trick him, I'm gonna try and cover up most of it so I don't have to pick so much. . . . All the other girls had to plow and cut pulpwood. We all had to work. The man [plantation owner] wasn't really too fair with him [her father], you know."[49] In order to help the family, Burton and her sisters would pick cotton and corn on a per diem basis for a local plantation owner.

> We picked corn, and they would pay us so much a pound. Now the cotton . . . he [the owner of the plantation] would say, "Oh I love to get those Johnson girls because they can pick a bale of cotton a day." My sisters, my older sisters could pick 350 pounds of cotton a day. I would pick 250 pounds. It's a bulb, I had to pick it out and it will stick you if you don't do it right.
> . . . We would stop at a store up there and get us lunch. We would be on the back of the truck by seven a.m. . . . We would get Ike and Mikes [a frosted cake with pink icing] . . . cheese, sardines, and crackers, and a big belly washer, that's what I call a big Pepsi. And that would be our lunch. And we would pick cotton all day until about three [p.m.] and he would bring us home and we would get washed up and we would do our chores at home.[50]

In addition to farming, Shubuta blacks often found work at one of the lumber companies surrounding the area. In the late nineteenth and early twentieth centuries there were as many as six lumber mills producing sawed lumber at one time.[51] This brought prosperity to the area during a time when the cotton farms were suffering from boll weevil damage. The largest lumber mill was the Brownlee Lumber Company that had the capacity to produce about 80,000 feet of lumber per day.[52] According to the 1930 United States Census, 16 percent of African American males who were household heads worked in various lumber mills in and around Shubuta.[53] The majority of these men were identified as laborers, but some were identified as log sawer, edgerman, chopper, and logger.[54] Two miles away in Wayne County there were also several small sawmills employing African Americans and one hardwood veneer mill where black women were employed to stack lumber for $1.00 a day.[55]

The 1930 United States Census reported a few African American heads of households in Shubuta holding jobs other than farming and sawmill labor. Some of these were preachers (3.3 percent), cooks (4.6 percent), laundry workers (4.6 percent), truck drivers (1.2 percent), and insurance agents (0.8 percent).[56] (see appendix 3).

Domestic work and farming were the major employment opportunities open to African American women in Mississippi during this time. All of the heads of households who reported their occupation as cooks (4.3 percent) and laundry (4.3 percent) were female. Exactly one-third, 33.3 percent, of the wives reported working with a private family. Cooks, maids, and nurses earned between $1.00 and $3.00 per week plus two meals a day.[57] Although the 1930 United States Census lists a small percentage of black women holding jobs, women during this time worked all day regardless of categorized employment. According to Girlie Ferguson, women in her family spent their days farming, cooking, canning fruits and vegetables, making and mending children's clothing, and basically doing whatever had to be done.[58]

Oral history interviews with Shubuta residents discuss older children and adolescents working on a per-diem basis despite the fact the United States Census did not show evidence of it. For example, Eddie Burton recalled the following:

My mother used to work for a lady called Mayfair Charmichel,
and she was the overseer of the welfare in Quitman. My mom
did the work for her. She was working for seven dollars a week.
Then when my mom stopped, I was nine years old and I started
taking care of her. I did cleaning. They had two bedrooms—no
three bedrooms—a kitchen, and a dining room, and two baths.
I cleaned that everyday. And on Saturday she discovered that I
could make biscuits. And on Saturday morning she wanted me
to come early and make biscuits for breakfast! And I said, "I'm
tired, I cook and clean . . . and baby-sit."[59]

This was all done after Eddie Burton attended school in the
mornings.

Despite the fact that the majority of African Americans in
Shubuta were forced into unskilled and service occupations, the
Federal Writers Project (FWP) workers for Clarke County seemed
surprised that black residents were unable to get ahead. In 1936,
the FWP workers reported the industrial progress of African
Americans in Shubuta.

Industrially, the Negro has not progressed so rapidly [in Clarke
County]; however, many of them learn little trades and do little extra
jobs. The following is a list of names of those Negroes who have
been issued licenses to carry on their trades in Clarke County.

Annie Thomas, Shubuta, Mississippi—Soft Drinks
Ethel Smith, Quitman, Mississippi—Soft Drinks
Dora Donald, Quitman, Mississippi—Lunch Stand
Edwin Price, Enterprise, Mississippi—Cobler [Cobbler]
Charles Moody, DeSoto, Mississippi—Barber
Nathan Hunter, West Enterprise, Mississippi—Café
Carrie Fisher, Shubuta, Mississippi—Soft Drinks
Ed Redford, Enterprise, Mississippi—Barber
Georgia Estes, Langsdale, Mississippi—Lunch Stand &
    Gen. Mdse.
Jonnah Portis, Stonewall, Mississippi—Lunch Stand
Jim House, Crandall, Mississippi—Lunch Stand[60]

To make employment matters worse, cotton farming became even more difficult for everyone in Shubuta during the first few decades of the twentieth century because of boll weevil infestations. African American tenant farmers were most likely hurt the worst because they operated on credit of future crop returns. Many tenant farmers had to absorb their landlord's losses as well as their own, "the advances furnished to the negroes can be held down to very low limits in case of necessity," in this case the necessity was the boll weevil.[61] In June of 1914, the *Mississippi Messenger* reported the condition of the cotton crop was the poorest since 1871 due to the boll weevil.[62] One year later, the newspaper reported that an additional 18,000 square miles of territory became infested.[63] The cotton pest continued to be a nuisance into the next decade. The *Mississippi Messenger* reported the following statistics on its front page on 21 December 1923 about the weevil infestations.

Weevil Effects Showing Strong

Boll weevil ravages in the South are showing up in cotton ginning reports and reports from the Census Bureau and these reports are comparatively small.

The Clarke [County] report of cotton ginners prior to November 14 amounted to 1746 bales against 3550 to same date last year, Lauderdale [County] this year ginned 3955, compared to 6071 last year, Wayne [County] this year ginned 1697 and 2725 last year; Jasper [County] ginned 2862 this year against 4880 last season.[64]

Boll weevil infestations added to the destitution of African American sharecroppers. These sharecroppers were the first ones to move away from crop destruction because they were affected the most. Grossman claims, "Neither black farm owners nor white farmers moved as readily as black tenants from infested areas, largely because the latter had the least latitude to react by changing the crop mix and were most subject to the impact of the boll weevil on the ability of credit."[65] Many of the migrants to Albany from Shubuta were sharecroppers.

DISCRIMINATION

W. E. B. Du Bois's *The Souls of Black Folk*, written in 1903, examined what it was like to be black and in the southern United States at the turn of the twentieth century.

> No wonder that Luke Black, slow, dull, and discouraged, shuffles to our carriage and talks hopelessly. Why should he strive? Every year finds him deeper in debt. How strange that Georgia, the world-heralded refuge of poor debtors, should bind her own to sloth and misfortune as ruthlessly as ever England did! The poor land groans with its birth-pains, and brings forth scarcely a hundred pounds of cotton to the acre, where fifty years ago it yielded eight times as much. Of his meager yield the tenant pays from a quarter to a third in rent, and most of the rest in interest on food and supplies bought on credit. Twenty years yonder sunken-cheeked, old black man has labored under that system, and now, turned day-laborer, is supporting his wife and boarding himself on his wages of a dollar and a half a week, received only part of the year.[66]

Discrimination in the South against African Americans was a major force that pushed migrants north. Racial biases and violence were the roots of many problems for blacks in regard to employment, justice, education, and socialization. Oral history interviews indicate that Shubuta was no different than the rest of the South when it came to discrimination against blacks.

The red artesian well, Shubuta's most famous landmark, is an artesian well that produces water the color of ice tea. For decades locals and travelers drank the red water for its medicinal properties. Doctors claimed that the red water would aid gout, acid indigestion, rheumatism, lumbago, a painful bladder, and constipation.[67] The earlier well had a wall dividing it. One side was for blacks; the other side was for whites. Girlie Ferguson, born in 1927, remembers an incident that occurred at the artesian well when she was a young girl revisiting Shubuta after moving to Albany.

> On Saturdays we went to town. We had gone to town and there was a well in this little town. The well had a faucet where the water came out and there were two sides to it. My Uncle Willie [McCann] went to one side and was drinking, so being from Albany and not knowing what goes on in the South that much, I went to the other side to drink. Then Uncle Willie gave me a slap across the face. I said, "What did you do that for?" He said, "You'd rather I do it than the white folks do it." So there was a black side and a white side.[68]

Eddie C. McDonald, an African American Shubuta resident who migrated to Denver, Colorado, and then returned to Shubuta to retire, recalled what it was like living in Shubuta in the 1930s.

> Back in those 1930s it was pretty rough back there. We had to work hard, and the schools weren't too easy to get to . . . there was very little work in Mississippi. . . . It took twelve families to sign in order for the electric company to bring lights our way. We had to walk one mile to get our mail because the mailman would not bring our mail to us. At that time you could not even see the light at the end of the tunnel. I think that's why I made up my mind to go and seek work. I left in 1954. It wasn't until the 1950s that things started to gel for us around here.[69]

When asked about what was different about Shubuta after returning home in 1994 to retire than when he left in 1954, McDonald had some interesting observations. "Now we [African Americans] can drink from the same fountain. When I left here there was a fountain with two pipes and water flowing out of each

side. One was for white and one was for black. When I came back
they had changed that and made it one faucet. . . . In 1954 when I
left here we could not vote at that time, but when I got to Denver,
in 1956, and had a chance to vote, I did, and I have been voting
ever since. And I have not missed hardly anything."[70] McDonald
also remembered that before he left Shubuta black people had to
guess the right number of jelly-beans in a large jar before they
were allowed to vote.[71]

Even the Works Progress Administration's historical surveys
comment on questionable disenfranchisement tactics in the area.
The whites first tried to influence who they thought were the more
intelligent blacks in the area to vote for the right candidate. When
this approach failed, the whites then questioned the rights of blacks
to vote at all. An argument ensured that the blacks' ballot was
destroyed. The Ku Klux Klan also terrorized African Americans
so they would be too afraid to vote.[72]

Another Shubuta resident, Willis McDonald, recalled
Mississippi's segregation during an interview. "Let me emphasize
this. There were two places down there in Shubuta that were
not segregated as far back as I can remember, those two doctors'
offices, Dr. Hand and Dr. Baydean. Everybody was in that same
room. Whoever came in and signs their name on that list and he
[Dr. Hand] took them as they came in. It was no one person was
over here and one over in this room. . . . The funeral home was not
segregated either, everybody was in the same thing."[73]

Reverend John Johnson from Shubuta told his son, McKinley
Johnson, that he had to leave Mississippi or he would have been
dead.[74] In an interview about his father, Johnson remembered, "He
would never raise a family under those discriminatory practices,
nor could he have a wife that would put up with those sharecropper
experiences. They were a touch above slavery. His independent
spirit would not let him stay there."[75] John Johnson felt that blacks
in Mississippi had such a hard life that after he established himself

in the North he returned south to transport blacks to Albany.

The Shubuta newspaper, the *Mississippi Messenger*, was published for the white citizens of the area. The majority of African American news that was reported dealt with lynching around Mississippi and when blacks did something unlawful. It was rare for African Americans to be praised or just plain reported about in the local Shubuta newspaper. Starting in December 1921, the *Mississippi Messenger* began running a front-page cartoon called "Hambone's Meditations," which served as a barometer for the general feelings of the white population toward blacks. These cartoons featured a white man in blackface who spoke in black dialect. The cartoon creators mocked African American work ethic, church, wives, law enforcement, and work relationships. These cartoons ran for about two years. One example in 16 December 1921 "Hambone's Meditations," featured a sloppily dressed man in blackface slowly fixing a fence. The caption read, "Talk bout lockin' folks up in jail fuh workin' on er-Sunday—ef dey eveh ketch me at dey kin' o'foolshness dey bettuh lock me in de crazy-house!!!!!"[76] Many of the issues that "Hambone's Meditations" scoffed at were reasons that oral history participants in this study cited for moving north.

The most atrocious form of discrimination took the form of lynching. Between 1882 and 1962, the state of Mississippi had 538 black lynchings, which was the highest number in the United States.[77] Lynching was also common in Shubuta. Usually when it occurred, it took place off a bridge at the end of East Street. Present-day Shubuta residents know this bridge as the "hanging bridge." One of the most horrifying incidents in Shubuta's history happened on 21 December 1918 when four black youths were accused of murdering a dentist named Dr. E. L. Johnson. The suspects, Andrew Clark, age fifteen; Major Clark, age twenty; Maggie Howze, age twenty; and Alma Howze, age sixteen, all pleaded innocent. The horrific account was published in the

National Association for the Advancement of Colored People's
(NAACP) race paper, the *Crisis*, and later picked up by an
independent Cincinnati, Ohio, paper known as the *Union*.

> It is common gossip around Shubuta that the murder was commit-
> ted by a white man who had a grudge against Johnson and who
> felt he could safely kill the dentist—and have blame fall on the
> Negro. At any rate, after subjecting the boy to extreme torture,
> a confession was secured from Major that he had committed the
> murder. At this, preparations for the lynching began. Major and
> Andrew Clark, Maggie and Alma Howze had all been arrested.
> After Major's confession they were taken to Shubuta for trial and
> placed in a little jail there. The mob secured the keys of the jail
> from the deputy sheriff in charge of the place without trouble,
> took out the prisoners and drove them to the place chosen for
> their execution, a little covered bridge over the Chickasawhay
> River. Four ropes were produced and four ends were tied to
> the girder on the underside of the bridge, while the other four
> ends were made into nooses and fastened securely around the
> necks of the four Negroes, who were standing on the bridge.
> Up until the last moment the Negroes protested their innocence
> and begged the mob not to be killed. Maggie Howze screamed
> and fought crying out, "I ain't guilty of killing the doctor and
> you oughtn't to kill me." In order to silence her cries one of the
> members of the mob seized a monkey wrench and struck her
> in the mouth with it, knocking her teeth out. She was also hit
> across the head with the same instrument, cutting a long gash.
> The four Negroes, when the ropes had been securely fastened
> about their necks, were taken bodily by the mob and thrown
> over the bridge. The younger girl and the two boys were killed
> instantly. Maggie Howze, however, who was a strong and vigor-
> ous woman, twice caught herself on the side of the bridge, thus
> necessitating her being thrown over the bridge three times. In
> town the next day, members of the mob told laughingly of how
> hard it had been to kill "that big black Jersey woman." The
> older girl of twenty was to become a mother in four months,
> while the younger was to have given birth to a child in two
> weeks. The sixteen-year-old prospective mother was killed on

Friday night and at the time of her burial on Sunday afternoon her unborn baby had not died. One could detect its movements in her womb.[78]

It is interesting that the report of this gruesome incident appeared in Cincinnati's newspaper, the *Union*. Perhaps this article was published in the Ohio paper to assure newly settled migrants that they made the correct choice in leaving the South. It is also possible, and probably more likely, that the article was published in northern African American papers to publicize the brutality of racist whites in the South and garner northern support against such acts.

The 1918 lynchings were not the only time the "hanging bridge" in Shubuta was used. In 1942, two fourteen-year-old black boys were hanged after being accused of an attempted rape of a thirteen-year-old white girl. Again the suspects were taken from their jail cells and brought to the bridge.[79] Another bridge, located one mile upriver from the Shubuta bridge, was the site of at least six similar lynchings.[80]

Discrimination, poor crop returns, dishonest landlords, poor educational opportunities, low wages, lynching, and segregation contributed to African Americans' desire to leave Mississippi during the Great Migration. Several families from Shubuta migrated to Albany. Many felt that Albany, and the North in general, was an asylum from southern racism. Upon arrival in the North, Shubuta residents were surprised to learn that conditions were not perfect. Albany had its own set of racial biases and discrimination.

CHAPTER 2

"God Led Me to Albany"

The Albany that Louis W. Parson discovered upon his arrival from the Deep South was a city on the move. The 1930 census placed the state capital's population at 127,412, with 98 percent white and 86 percent native born.[1] About half, 52 percent, of all white families lived in nuclear households while 17 percent lived in extended households, 12 percent lived in augmented households, 3 percent lived in extended and augmented households, and 7.4 percent lived in one-parent households.[2]

The late 1920s found Albany's infrastructure modernizing and its population dispersing beyond the traditional neighborhoods. A new City Planning Commission was established in 1927 to purchase new land for proper highways, extend city streets into developing neighborhoods, and install modern traffic lights and controls. Buses were quickly replacing trolleys as the chief mode of transporting workers from home to job.

With an increasing population and improvements in transportation, city planners and private developers began addressing housing needs. By the late 1920s, the borders of the city began pushing further westward, away from the Hudson River and original core of settlement. This era found rows of flats developing for working-class families along Delaware and New Scotland avenues. These double-family structures offered a home and rental income for their owners, often members of the extended family pooling resources. Albany's wealthy continued to build out

31

Western Avenue, extending the Pine Hills neighborhood.[3] Family farms and pine barrens could be found beyond all of Albany's newest neighborhoods. Roughly 60 percent of white families in Albany rented their homes, while 38 percent owned their homes.[4] Furthermore, 39 percent of the white population had no children, 25 percent had one child, 19.5 percent had two children, 7.6 percent had three children, 4.7 percent had four children, and 3.4 percent had five or more children.[5]

New arrivals to Albany found housing in Albany's oldest neighborhoods along the river. These neighborhoods were composed of row houses broken into apartments and shops. Once fashionable, these areas became worn after generations of new arrivals to Albany established themselves and then with success moved on to better quarters and neighborhoods.[6] Albany continued its historical role as a crossroads of trade and commerce. Governor Alfred E. Smith created the Albany Port District and a thirty-mile channel was dredged in the Hudson River. When the Port of Albany officially opened in 1932, it contained the world's largest single-unit grain elevator and was capable of handling 85 percent of the world's oceangoing ships. In the same year, the Dunn Memorial Bridge opened, offering a modern thoroughfare for crossing the Hudson River, with its designers boasting that it could handle 30,000 vehicles daily. Albany also served as the intersection of six major railroads and the starting point of the revamped New York State Barge Canal System. The increasing power of air transport brought about the creation of Lindbergh Field in 1928, the nation's first city-owned airport.

Parson soon would have discovered that machine politics ruled the new city he would call home. By the late 1920s, the Democratic Party achieved a two-to-one advantage over the city's Republicans in voter registration. Just ten years earlier, the Republican Party had a three-to-one edge over the Democrats. The O'Connell-Corning Democratic machine ran politics in Albany County until Mayor Erastus Corning, 2nd, died in 1983.[7]

The full effects of the Depression began to be felt on Albany in the early 1930s. Total wages fell over 27 percent and the city was aiding 2,200 families with fuel, food, and rent assistance. The city also began its own public works projects as a way of helping unemployed Albanians and assisting local contractors. During this time, Philip Livingston School was built; the Alcove and Basic reservoirs were built, along with 144 miles of paved streets. Albany was also fortunate to be the seat of state government, for state employment helped Albany survive the Depression better than many other northeastern industrial cities such as Schenectady.

In William Kennedy's book, *O Albany!* the author summarizes what happened to Albany during the Great Migration.

> After World War I the large influx of poor rural Southern Negroes changed the world for longtime residents. Because the newcomers settled in the South End, Arbor Hill became the desirable place for the Negro elite and those with upward mobility. The Arbor Hill Community Center, whose forerunner was established in 1928, became the liaison between the Negro and white communities. The Negro population of the city had gone from 1,239 in 1920 to an estimated 2,100 in 1930, and a sizable Negro neighborhood had been created in the South End. The Reverend John Johnson, in 1963 pastor of Franklin Street's Church of God in Christ, remembered the neighborhood's being below South Pearl Street, from Hudson Avenue to Schuyler Street, although Irish and Italians and Jews also occupied the same areas.
>
> "That was the Depression," he remembered, "and they could only rent the cheapest kind of houses. Then the work started picking up, and more and more came in. During the war they flooded in like water."[8]

The division between the northern-born blacks and the newly arrived poor southern blacks discussed in this excerpt was an issue in cities throughout the North. These transplanted southerners brought their religious beliefs, food, ideas, families, and lifestyle with them, changing the face of Albany forever.

Table 2. Albany's Black Population, 1890 to 1970

Year	Total Population	Black	Percent of Total Population
1890	94,923	1,122	1.2%
1900	94,151	1,178	1.3%
1910	100,253	1,037	1.0%
1920	113,344	1,239	1.1%
1930	127,412	2,324	1.8%
1940	130,577	2,929	2.2%
1950	134,325	5,785	4.3%
1960	129,726	10,972	8.5%
1970	115,781	14,930	12.9%

Source: 11th through 19th United States Censuses

FAMILY STRUCTURE

According to the 1930 United States Census, 39.7 percent of the African American households in Albany were considered nuclear, 12.3 percent were extended, 26.5 percent were augmented, 4.8 percent were extended and augmented, 11.1 percent were head only, and 5.4 percent were one parent households.[9] Exactly 50 percent of the one-parent households were the result of the death of a spouse.

The largest differences between household composition in Albany, New York, and Shubuta, Mississippi, were in the extended household and augmented household classifications. In Shubuta, 26.6 percent of African American households were extended. In Albany only 12.3 percent of African Americans lived in extended households, since small city dwellings and industrial employment made it difficult for extended families to live together. Also, older members of migrant families often stayed behind because they were set in their ways or felt they were too old for such a big

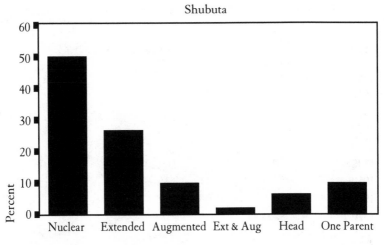

Shubuta

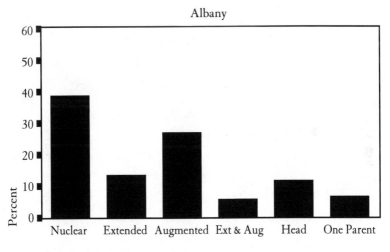

Albany

Source: United States Bureau of the Census, *Fifteenth Census of the United States Taken in 1930*

Figure 1. Comparison of Household Composition of African American Families in Shubuta and Albany, 1930

lifestyle change. In a rural, agricultural-based setting, families lived in homes and relatives usually could help with chores associated with a self-sufficient rural lifestyle, such as farm chores, making clothing, and woodworking. Another difference in household composition was that in Albany 26.5 percent of blacks lived in augmented households, while in Shubuta only 7.8 percent of the families were augmented households. Again, city families are more inclined to have boarders than rural families because urban living is associated with a higher cost of living; boarders were often an economic necessity. Many of these boarders were individuals who came north in search of economic opportunities, established themselves, and then sent for their families to join them.

In Albany, 59.5 percent had no children, while in Shubuta it was 38.3 percent. The percentages of black families having between one and four children per family in both areas were nearly equal. Changes between the two areas became great as family size increased. In Albany, 4.0 percent of black families had five to six children, while in Shubuta it was 11.0 percent. In Albany only 0.6 percent had between seven and ten children, while in Shubuta it was 9.0 percent. It is not surprising that rural southern families, both black and white, had more children than northern city families, due to readily available food from their farms and the fact that with extended family members around more children could be raised. Also, having extra children meant additional help with chores and fieldwork.

RACE ORGANIZATIONS

Despite the fact that African Americans made up only a small percentage of Albany's population, there were at least three social groups working to improve their housing conditions, educational opportunities, and race relations. For example, the Maria C. Lawton

Civic and Cultural Club was organized in April 1919 "for the purpose of promoting community service, educational advancement, inter-cultural relations and personal self development."[10] It was a branch of the Empire State Federation of Women's Clubs and the first black organization in Albany actively involved with race relations. In its early years, the M. C. Lawton Club centered its efforts and financial support on the African American churches, senior citizens of the community, families in need of emergency assistance, and children.[11]

The Albany Inter-Racial Council was another organization that strove to help African Americans in Albany. The Albany Inter-Racial Council began in May 1928 "to investigate and study the social conditions existing among the various races in the city of Albany, with particular reference to the Negro; to plan programs of social improvements based upon the findings of such studies and investigations; and to improve the relationship of the races."[12] The idea to establish the Albany Inter-Racial Council occurred when James Weldon Johnson came to Albany on 28 March 1928 to speak at the First Unitarian Church. When the audience arrived at the church to hear Johnson's lecture, they voluntarily sat with their own racial groups; blacks on one side of the church, whites on the other. After Johnson gave his lecture titled "The Negro Problem in America," a woman visiting from the South claimed that she was surprised to find segregation at this meeting in Albany.[13] Apparently this statement stirred up the audience's emotions and the moderator announced if anyone present was interested in the possible formation of an inter-racial council in Albany, they should meet for a few minutes after the program. A small group of both blacks and whites assembled and two months later the council was formally established.[14]

One of the biggest impacts the Albany Inter-Racial Council had on the city of Albany's African American population and their history was its commission of a survey entitled *The Negro*

Population—Albany, New York—by Dr. Ira De A. Reid, director of the Department of Research and Investigations, National Urban League (NUL), in December 1928. The survey was comprehensive and detailed, discussing housing, healthcare, crime, education, recreation, and religion of Albany's African Americans. The council used the NUL survey as a springboard for its first activities and programs. For example the survey recommended that "an administrative social organization, inter-racial in its directing constituency, be created; such an organization to have as its purpose the amelioration of social difficulties affecting the Negro, and a coordination of the social efforts of churches, clubs and fraternal organizations."[15] As a result, in March 1929 the Inter-Racial Council secured the services of James H. Baker, Jr., as its executive secretary and opened up its first office on Chapel Street. The officers then approached the Community Chest, the present-day United Way, and secured money for the council as a chest member.[16] The NUL survey is one of the few existing published accounts of African American life in Albany in the beginning of the twentieth century.

The Albany branch of the National Association for the Advancement of Colored People (NAACP) was founded in 1935 in response to perceived unnecessary police violence toward African Americans. Albany's first NAACP meeting was held in February 1935 at the Israel African Methodist Church located at 381 Hamilton Street. The first president of the branch was Dr. William Fletcher Brown, an Albany dentist who personally obtained many of the signatures necessary to warrant a charter from the national organization.[17] The primary goals for Albany NAACP members were equal access to housing, education, employment, and an end to police brutality. The organization succeeded at encouraging department stores to hire black clerks in Albany. It supported the national antilynching laws, pressed for integration of the United States Armed Forces, and brought the Scottsboro Boys to Albany in 1936 to tell their story.[18] The Albany NAACP used peaceful means of lobbying, protests, and litigation to achieve its goals.[19]

These social organizations, along with local churches, were successful in helping African Americans with several aspects of daily life. Harriet Van Vranken, a socially active member of Albany's black elite, commented on race organizations as noted in William Kennedy's book *O! Albany.* " 'From around 1915 on, you really saw the Negroes getting together, organizing for the betterment of the group, and the stimulus came mainly from older men and women'—men such as her father and Abe Myers, who worked as a porter, and William H. Johnson, who was a barber. 'Those men had been very active in the Underground Railroad [*sic*] and they continued to fight for Negro rights and press the young people to get an education.' "[20] It appears that these organizations were at least somewhat successful. Girlie Ferguson, who moved to Albany, New York, from Hattiesburg, Mississippi, in May 1939, recalled the South End neighborhood where she grew up.

> We lived on Dongan Avenue and I can remember at least six [African American] families that lived on Dongan Avenue. There were some [African Americans] that lived on Herkimer Street, some that lived on Franklin Street, they were all around. It was a community of Italians and blacks that lived in the area we lived in when we first moved to Albany. I had many Italian friends, even through high school and junior high school. One of my best friends was Italian. . . . In junior high school my best friend was Rosemary Shirello. I had another little girlfriend, she wasn't Italian, and her name was Rae Cuebus. Rae and I used to go shopping so we could dress alike. I had friends of all nationalities when I was going to school.[21]

HOUSING

Housing was an issue for many Africans Americans who migrated to Albany from the 1920s on. In 1930, the majority (85.8 percent) of African Americans lived in rental households, while only 11.1 percent owned their own homes.[22] According to the 1930 United

States Census, 65 percent of the black population lived in wards 3, 5, 7, and 12.[23] Wards 3 and 5 are in the area known as the South End. During the 1920s, 1930s, and 1940s Italians, Jews, and blacks occupied the South End. By the late 1950s the area was almost entirely black. Reverend John Johnson, a pastor in the South End from Shubuta, remembered, "That area [the South End] waned as south to north migration intensified and by 1930 a definite Negro ghetto had been created."[24] Johnson also remembered it encompassed the area below South Pearl, roughly from Hudson Avenue to Schuyler Street (see appendix 4).[25]

Geneva Conway, an African American who moved to Albany from Mississippi with her family in 1944, remembered growing up in the South End.

> We lived in the South End, we moved from Bleecker Street around the corner to Dongan Avenue, our own place. We lived in what was really a multiethnic neighborhood. You had people of the Czechoslovakian, Yugoslavian group, you had the Jews and you had the blacks. Very few Irish, I believe they were in north or west Albany. So in the South End it was the blacks, the Jews, and the Italians. I don't know what it was about us; maybe it was because all of us were so poor. We did not have time to fight one another as races—we had to survive. And I don't want to paint a rosy picture here with you that there was no racism, but all of us kids, if we fought one another, we fought because you were from uptown. We didn't fight you because you were white. If you came from below the Strand Theater, you were in trouble. If you went above the Strand Theater, going towards Arbor Hill, you were in trouble. Now we didn't care what color you were, you were in trouble.[26]

The poorest people in Albany lived in the South End during this time, which by default consisted of the newest immigrant and migrant groups to the city. This area was also home to many bars, gambling houses, and prostitutes. According to William Kennedy's historical reminiscences, Albany was second only to Chicago in its level of prostitution. Of the 1,200 women in the South End, 400 were streetwalkers, he claimed.[27]

In 1928, the National Urban League (NUL) studied African American housing concerns. The survey reported that the wards where the largest numbers of blacks lived tended to have the smallest population, due to the fact that these wards were no longer desirable residential areas and were being invaded by businesses and factories.[28] Furthermore these sections showed the greatest decreases in the number of available family dwellings between 1910 and 1920.[29] The NUL described one of the black sections of town along the Hudson River: "In this district many of the frame houses are untenable; brick walls are cracked and in need of painting; many of the rooms need artificial light all day long; toilets connect with the kitchen (often with no door in between); halls, yards, toilets are shared by many families; the district area is flanked on one side by the "closed" red light district which is patrolled by policemen, especially assigned to that duty, for twenty-four hours a day"[30] (see appendix 5). This survey also collected specific information on 255 African American homes throughout Albany. The NUL report claimed that the constant influx of new African Americans to Albany was a consistent factor causing increased difficulty finding housing for blacks, increased rents, overcrowding, and unsanitary conditions[31] (see appendix 6). If it was difficult to rent a home in Albany if you were African American, it was almost impossible to buy one. According to several migrants the only real estate company that would deal with blacks was Albert and Kersh Realty.[32]

South End resident Patricia Beebee remembers the conditions for African Americans in the South End. "I can remember single women going up and down First Street not being able to find a room. There were a lot of rooming houses going on in my neighborhood and that was the first time I can remember anything about segregation and discrimination because there were women and families that could not find apartments. That was the first time I realized our people were having a struggle. . . . Those people who had homes, their rooms were chopped up into little rooms."[33]

According to James Stamper, an African American who migrated to Schenectady in 1930 from Atlanta, Georgia, the Capital District, on a whole, had poor housing conditions for migrants. He remembered trying to find housing upon arrival.

> It was very disappointing for me; in 1930 . . . we came in the summer right after school closed. But coming to Schenectady was a real shock to me when we looked around for housing. It was almost impossible to find any housing that was decent. I came from Atlanta where my dad was a bricklayer . . . he built a big ten-room house on the east side and we were living comfortably. Coming to Schenectady you just couldn't find anything like that and if you found it, they wouldn't rent it to you. It was impossible to buy; we just didn't have the money. It was one of the most discouraging experiences that I can remember when coming to Schenectady. My mother and all of us—there were ten of us—five boys and five girls—we were just not able to find housing. We lived with my uncle for a while, until we were able to find housing. When we did [find housing,] it was really not adequate and it took several years and several tries until we were able to get decent housing. . . . This was rental; we did not buy a house until 1950.[34]

Despite the hardships of trying to find adequate housing in the North, Stamper claims that living conditions for African Americans were better in Schenectady, on the whole, than they were in Atlanta.[35]

Leon Dukes, an African American whose parents migrated from South Carolina, recalled his family's experiences obtaining housing in Albany.

> My parents' first house as a couple was on Sheridan Avenue in Albany. Rented by a lady named Mrs. Swartz and she owned

most of the houses on Sheridan Avenue and Orange Street. She specialized in renting to African Americans from the South. I remember she used to come around all dressed in black and collect the rent. And then when my parents went to buy a house up on Livingston Avenue, close to Northern Boulevard, which was a primary Irish community, there was a lot of resistance. There was one other black family in the neighborhood, but they had no children. So the threat was that we were coming with children. . . . They bought their first house for $5,000 at the site now where you see Stewart's on Northern Boulevard. They had fifty dollars to put down on the house and the only bank that would give them a mortgage was Cohoes Saving Bank. My mother said that was the only bank that would give blacks an opportunity . . . it did not matter how much you had in your savings account.[36]

William Fletcher Brown, one of Albany's first black dentists, was able to start a dental practice, but could not rent space anywhere. Born in Lauderdale, Mississippi, in 1900, Brown came to Albany beginning in 1921 for summer work between semesters at Howard University in Washington, D.C. Brown was a Pullman porter and chose Albany because of its central location.[37] From Albany, a train porter could accept jobs that took him to New York City, Boston, Montreal, and Buffalo. After graduation in 1929 Brown moved to Chicago where he passed the Illinois State Board Dental Examinations. Shortly after, he left Chicago because of high unemployment. Friends encouraged him to move back to Albany where opportunities were supposed to be better.[38]

Brown moved back in 1932, passed the New York State Board Dental Examinations, and attempted to open a practice in Albany. No one would rent Dr. Brown space in the downtown business section on State Street and North Pearl. Dr. James A. Spencer, an African American physician and friend, helped him rent space in his building on Central Avenue. After Brown bought all of his dental equipment, the building's landlord refused him space. The landlord's reason was "because of what neighbors would say with two black professionals in the same building on one of the city's main thoroughfares."[39] With all of his equipment and no place to put it, he opened his first practice in his home at 90 Second Street where he lived with a couple, Mr. and Mrs. William Parker. In 1934, he opened an office at 146 South Pearl Street and Bleecker Street. Dr. Brown worked until his retirement in 1980.[40] He was the first president of Albany's NAACP branch in 1935.

Reverend John (Jack) Johnson and his family lived in several different apartments throughout the South End until they were able to buy a home on 58 Rensselaer Street. Reverend McKinley Johnson, John Johnson's son, recalled the family's history. "We had very poor experiences. We lived right down the street on Green . . . Dongan Avenue, Bassett Avenue; I was born on Bleecker Street. We always lived in the South End. We lived on Ferry Street. As time moved on we moved to Rensselaer Street—the top of Rensselaer Street on the corner of Pearl Street."[41] The Johnson family had trouble renting apartments, so they decided to buy a house. "It was a very holy home. I mean holes all in the walls. It was at 58 Rensselaer Street. He [John Johnson] did not have a lot of money and no one wanted to rent, so he purchased a dilapidated house. It was an Albert and Kersh no-down-payment house. I think my father worked out a deal with them."[42] John Johnson was able to use his handyman skills to fix up the house. Eventually, these skills led to future employment opportunities for Johnson. At one time Johnson had ten homes that he was repairing for black families.[43]

Not every African American family had a difficult time in securing housing upon arrival in Albany. It was common for new migrants to live with family or friends for a time after their arrival. Often, after a family moved north, letters were sent home encouraging others to join them. James Grossman discussed this phenomenon in his book on migration to Chicago. "More than any other advertisement, agent, or publication, letters spoke to

black southerners in their own language and addressed their major
concerns. . . . A man who promised to tell his friends how he fared
needed to write only one letter, which was then shared by all."[44]
If a migrant did not have family or friends to live with, he or she
could rent a room or live with another family. Almost one-third
(31.2 percent) of all African American households in Albany in
1930 had boarders, lodgers, or roomers.[45]

Many of the Albany civic organizations, both black and white,
made African American housing a premier issue. For example, in
1929 the Albany Inter-Racial Council proposed to help African
Americans improve housing conditions by recommending that
blacks be instructed in the technique of home buying, creating
a semi-philanthropic enterprise to make additional residences
available for blacks, seeking the cooperation of real estate dealers
to minimize the difficulties faced by blacks when looking for
better housing conditions, and by forming block associations
among black residents to increase interest in the particular sections
where they lived.[46]

The M. C. Lawton Club made African American housing
conditions one of its premier issues in the late 1920s and 1930s.
Club members believed "Better homes mean better children, better
children mean better men and women, better men and women
mean better citizens, and better citizens mean a better America."[47]
The M. C. Lawton Club's housing investigation was similar to the
NUL, Inter-Racial Council, and the NAACP reports. In July 1928
the Housing Committee headed by Christina G. Harris, reported
the following conditions:

1. Renting of "down-at-the-heel" property to our people.
2. Abnormal rents.
3. Gross insanitation.
4. Cellar living.
5. Windowless rooms.

6. Overcrowding.
7. Outside toilets.
8. Water in the yards.
9. Much disrepair.[48]

Club members felt that education was the best way to solve this issue. The M. C. Lawton Club's housing committee gave talks to women's clubs and missionary societies on the housing conditions for blacks in Albany. The club also educated African Americans on the duties and obligations of landlords and tenants, sanitary science, and hygienic housekeeping. At the end of 1928, the M. C. Lawton Club held a contest for homeowners and tenants; prizes were given for the best-kept homes and yards[49] (see appendix 7).

EMPLOYMENT

Employment opportunity was one of the major reasons why southern African Americans migrated north. World War I caused immigration from Europe to taper off, thus creating job opportunities in the North. There was an increased demand for labor and few immigrants to supply it, so many manufacturers dropped their racial biases and hired blacks for the first time. However, the majority of Albany's migrant population did not come north as a result of war production employment opportunities. Albany's African American population only increased from 1,037 to 1,239 between 1910 and 1920.[50] Its large increase in black population occurred from 1920 to 1930 (1,239 to 2,324), 1940 to 1950 (2,929 to 5,785), and 1950 to 1960 (5,785 to 10,972).[51] The 1920 to 1930 African American population increase could be the result of poor crop returns in the South in the 1920s due to a series of bad droughts, floods, and the boll weevil cotton infestation. Agricultural setbacks coupled with the onset of the Depression most likely caused poor southerners to be destitute. Many moved north because their economic situation could not get any worse.

The 1928 NUL survey identified three employment opportunities that drew African Americans to the Capital Region. The first was Albany's central location between New York, New England, and Canadian summer resorts. Thus, Albany was home to a transient group of black domestic and summer resort workers. Second was the proximity of many brickyards in the Hudson Valley. These businesses began hiring blacks in the early 1920s. The last factor was Hudson River projects that brought blacks to the Albany area, such as the Dunn Memorial Bridge connecting Albany and Rensselaer counties.[52] Additional employment opportunities for African Americans in the area were the result of the New York Central and Delaware and Hudson railroad headquarters, and consequently, their repair facilities.

The Capital Region was home to several large manufacturing industries such as Albany Felt Company, Ludlum Steel Company, Albany Packing Company, and J. B. Lyon Company. The 1928 NUL survey reported that these five industries employed over 25,000 workers, but only 124 of them were black.[53] The report noted, "While no industry using Negro labor expresses dissatisfaction with it, three qualified their fitness for certain types of work only."[54] The industrial work that blacks were allowed to do was usually the hardest, hottest, coldest, dirtiest work available. This was true in cities and factories across the North.

During the 1930s, unemployment in Albany was high as the Great Depression progressed. By November 1930, it was estimated that 25 percent of Albany's total workforce was unemployed.[55] Reverend John Johnson remembered, "That was the depression and jobs were even worse than they are now [in 1967]. That meant they [blacks] could rent only the cheapest kind of houses. . . . And it stayed pretty near the same from 1930 to 1939, then the work started picking up and more and more [black people] came in.

During the war [World War II] they flooded in like water and kept right on, up till now."[56] During this time the railroads and the Port of Albany project helped supply some of the few jobs available for blacks and whites. The Port of Albany building project began in 1925 and was finished in 1932. Workers dredged a twenty-seven-foot-deep, thirty-mile-long channel up the Hudson River that allowed most oceangoing ships to sail from New York City to Albany. Also the New York Central Railroad and the Delaware & Hudson Railroad laid a twenty-five-mile web of track to aid in the movement of materials in and out of the port, creating jobs in the process.[57]

According to the 1930 United States Census the top five occupations for African American heads of households living in Albany were laborer (26.7 percent), porter (15.0 percent), maid/housekeeper (5.3 percent), chauffeur (2.5 percent), and cook (2.3 percent).[58] Only 53 (11.1 percent) out of the 479 heads of households claimed no employment. The top five industries that these heads of households worked in were railroad (18 percent), private family (9.8 percent), construction (6.3 percent), garage (5.0 percent), and building (4.8 percent).[59] The majority (86.4 percent) of these jobs were wage employment, while only 2.9 percent of these workers were employed on their own account. There were no African Americans listed in the "employer" category.[60] These statistics indicate that blacks in Albany, as in other northern cities, held jobs at the bottom of the socioeconomic hierarchy. The majority, 76.3 percent, of those heads of households who were married did not list their wives as working. The wives who did work found the majority of their employment in domestic trades such as cleaning/housekeeping (10.1 percent), cook (4.4 percent), laundry (2.2 percent), maid in hotel (1.6 percent), and dressmaker (.9 percent).[61]

Albany's occupational structure somewhat reflects that of other northern cities during the Great Migration. Only 1.5 percent of black household heads were classified as professionals, 1.9

percent were classified as proprietary, 4.5 percent were classified as skilled, 3.2 were classified as semiskilled, and 77.5 percent were classified as unskilled laborers.[62] In larger cities like Chicago, Cleveland, and New York more blacks were spread throughout the occupational categories because these cities had a large enough black population to support all-black institutions such as shops, schools, hospitals, and insurance companies, and to elect black politicians. Albany did not have a large enough black population to support separate establishments, therefore Albany's blacks had to work in subservient positions within white institutions.

Although there was not a definite business area for the black population, there were a few African American owned businesses scattered throughout Albany. According to the 1928 NUL survey Albany blacks owned and operated one printing shop, one stationary store, three tailor shops, one secondhand furniture store, one service company, two barber shops, two pool rooms, one house-cleaning business, one real estate business, and one restaurant.[63]

Oral history interviews reveal that it was hard for African American males to find work in the Capitol Region. James Stamper, who came to Schenectady in 1930, got his first job at the Van Cuyler Hotel because his uncle was the headwaiter there. The only job in the hotel open to Stamper was in the food department, which paid $1.00 a day, but they charged $.10 a day to clean his uniform jacket.[64] Stamper worked at the Van Cuyler until he got a job with the General Electric Company. He felt that the General Electric Company was very discriminatory because it was difficult for blacks to get jobs of any consequence. Most of the employment given to African Americans at that time was custodial work.[65] Stamper recalls how he was able to secure employment at the General Electric Company.

> I applied many times [at the General Electric Company] and they would tell me that they kept these applications on file for

six months, and they would say come back in six months if you don't hear from us and we will have you apply again. And I applied many times, I go down and they would say, "sorry, we're not hiring." So I would make another application, leave it, and go to work. I would continually go back, I wanted them to know that I wanted to get into industry because there was a lot of industrialization in this area, but to get a good job in industry was very difficult. I went back time and again until about 1942; I was very desperate then because that's when they started putting everybody in the service. I said I am gonna have to get inside somewhere. Finally they told me there was a job available as a material handler, I had never heard of such a thing in my entire life, what was that? The government had control of all the material because of the war effort . . . it was really a glorified porter's job. I had to go around and check materials at all the machines and make sure the porters were putting the different kinds of scrap metal into the right barrels, my job was to take record of that and send it down to the foundry. . . . But, when they decided to give me the job, they called me in, and they had all of my applications clipped right together. At the top of the application there was a red circle: AMERICAN NEGRO. I found they did not destroy all those applications; it was a way of keeping track of who was who. Because in those days it seemed to have meant so much more to them who you were rather than what you were going to do for the company.[66]

Stamper ended up taking the job at the General Electric Company and continued working there, slowly moving up in positions for over thirty-five years.

Some families arrived in Albany by following employment from job to job. Leon Dukes's family, originally from South Carolina, moved to Albany because his uncle got a job working on the Holland Tunnel in New York City.[67] Dukes remembered his uncle's remark about working on the Holland Tunnel: "For a person who can't swim, I sure worked where I shouldn't have been."[68] After the job in New York City was over, Dukes's uncle moved to Albany to work on the bridge that connected Albany and Rensselaer. When the bridge was completed he and his family were left in Albany without a job, so he was forced to do what day work he could find. Dukes's uncle heard about day work helping unload banana boats at the Port of Albany and at Allegheny Ludlum Steel. At Ludlum Steel the foreman came outside in the morning and picked day workers, but they never picked black men to do the work.[69]

Leon Dukes also remembers employment for African Americans being so tough to obtain in the late 1930s that at the first word of a job, several people would show up for it. Deacon Landy Thomas, a black migrant from South Carolina, was a porter at Allegheny Ludlum Steel. One day when he was cleaning his boss's office, the boss told him, "Landy, I want to hire a colored boy. Why don't you tell some colored boys to come out here for a job? In particular, I want to hire that tall one that comes out here everyday."[70] The tall man referred to was Reverend Brewington Stiney (eventually a preacher at Bethel Baptist Church in Troy, New York), from Greedyville, South Carolina. Dukes's father, Reverend Stiney, and a man named Smitty were all having dinner together when Landy Thomas stopped by to tell Stiney that he should go to Ludlum Steel for work. Dukes's father and Smitty heard about the job so they decided to try and get one too.

> They [Dukes's father and Smitty] got up early the next morning and they only had one nickel between the both of them, so neither could ride the bus. They walked from Albany to Watervliet. At that time Allegheny Ludlum Steel had dormitories and a cafeteria. My father said by the time they got to the cafeteria they were no longer black men; they were white men because the frost and the snow covered them up. . . . They got into the line and Reverend Stiney was picked to work for the first time after going out there for several weeks to wait in line. . . . Smitty got a job the next day and my father went three days in a row and never got picked.[71]

Reverend Stiney and Smitty ended up getting jobs grinding steel, which was one of the hardest and most dangerous jobs at the plant.

Geneva Conway remembers, "When my parents came here, it was easier for my mother to get a job. My mother went to work first at BASF, which was GAF (both plastic manufacturing companies) at that time in Rensselaer."[72] It was easier for African American women than African American men to get work in the Albany area because jobs as domestic workers were usually available. According to the 1930 United States Census 17.9 percent out of the 23.7 percent of African American wives who worked, did so in the domestic industry.[73] Also, during World War II many women, both black and white, worked in local factories such as the Watervliet Arsenal, while men were engaged in military service.

EDUCATION

African Americans were relegated to the poorest and most dilapidated schools in Albany. The blacks and poor whites were taught in schools built in the nineteenth century and staffed by teachers whose lifestyles were very different from their own.[74] In 1910, only 116 African Americans between the ages of seven and nineteen attended school in Albany. The number of black children attending school increased to 143 in 1920 and 261 in 1928, not surprising considering the black population increased in these years also.[75] By 1928, there had only been four black teachers in the history of the Albany public school system, and the New York State College for Teachers in Albany, which was the training school for a majority of Albany's teachers, had no black students in 1928 and had had no black graduates since 1925.[76]

According to the 1928 NUL survey, there were 261 African American children distributed in fifteen of the twenty-nine Albany public schools.[77] The school with the largest numbers of black students (forty-five) was Public School 15, located on Herkimer and Franklin streets in Albany's South End neighborhood. Public

School 15 was ethnically diverse during this time, with African American, Polish, Jewish, Spanish, Italian, Chinese, Gypsy, and native-born white students attending.[78] African American school attendance in Albany must have been low because in the spring of 1928 the M. C. Lawton Club launched a "stay in school" campaign aimed at black high school students. The club claimed there were a large number of black students who left school at both the junior high and high school levels.[79] The M. C. Lawton Club held meetings for both the parents and students discussing the importance of education for blacks as a group.[80]

Black students may not have attended school because their families moved around from job to job, making it difficult to stay enrolled in one school. Also, many older children did not always attend school because they worked to help their family's financial situation. Lastly, black students, especially those who recently migrated from the South, felt much racism and discrimination from the almost all-white schools in Albany. Because of segregation in the South, migrant children were used to attending all-black schools with black instructors. Attending a mixed classroom was probably terrifying for many children. Geneva Conway felt this way. "When we came here [Albany], it was kind of a shock to me because in class there might have been one or two blacks, but where I had come from [Shubuta] there were classes of all blacks. When I went to college [at the State University of New York at Cobleskill for nutrition] there were two blacks in the whole class and I was the darkest one there. The other one's [the other black student's] eyes were gray, she could have passed [as a white person]."[81]

An annual example of racism in the Albany public schools that occurred at Hackett Junior High School until 1928 was a minstrel show. In March 1928, the M. C. Lawton Club petitioned Hackett Junior High's Principal, John A. Naughton, to stop the minstrel show. The club stated, "there was nothing of educational value in a minstrel show, and such an entertainment acted adversely to the best interests of the Negro. It spreads false ideas, and impresses upon the white group unfavorably concepts and generalities already held by them. It mocked the very ideals, which the Negro holds dear—his virtue, his church, and his home. The Negro student would of course suffer humiliation."[82] Principal Naughton agreed with the club and cancelled the show, promising "that no activities would be held in school which would create discomfort to any group of the student body."[83]

James Stamper was impressed with the educational system in Schenectady, New York, and he enjoyed going to school with black and white students because it was so different from his segregated schools in Atlanta, Georgia. Stamper felt racism in school every now and then. "It was there [racism], but not overtly. If you were on top of some particular topic or study, it seems to me that the black students did not get the credit that the other students were getting. You had to be very far out in front because there was an effort to denigrate your ability."[84] Geneva Conway had similar feelings when it came to school. "If a black person was on top of it [a subject or project at school] all of a sudden it was not too important. If blacks were doing a better job, then not so much importance was placed on it. It might have even gone away altogether."[85] Conway also recalled that "in high school I think there was some segregation [discrimination] as far as I was concerned. There were some prizes I think should have went to me, but went the other way. But because my parents were focused on me getting an education, I did not fight those battles."[86]

Education for black children in Albany during this time was far from optimal. Black students in Albany did not have the opportunity to work with teachers and advisors of their own race and backgrounds. Oral history interviews reveal that black students were not encouraged to achieve academically, opportunities for advancement were restricted, and there were few programs designed to help black students in Albany reach their full potential.

BLACK CHURCHES

Prior to the Great Migration, Albany's African American churchgoing population either attended white churches or one of the two local black churches.[87] The Israel African Methodist Episcopal (A.M.E.) Church, organized in 1787, was the oldest and largest black church in Albany. By 1928, it had more than three hundred members.[88] The Morning Star Baptist Church, the other local black church, claimed a membership of two hundred and an edifice valued at $40,000 in 1928.[89]

With the influx of southern black migrants, between 1920 and 1928 at least seven new African American churches were established in Albany.[90] The new churches usually had small congregations, no consecrated buildings to worship in, and assembled in private residences or store buildings. These "storefront" churches began to appear all over Albany, particularly in the South End, in the 1920s, catering to the newest members of the black community who were used to the informal, emotional, preacher-orientated churches of the rural South. Despite the establishment of these new churches, the 1928 NUL survey reported that "Though the church is the dominant in social control among the Negro population it has been ineffective in its activity. A very large portion of the population never attends any church, while ministers seem to maintain that, so far as the Negro population is concerned, Albany is not a 'church town.' "[91] Furthermore, in a 1964 *Albany Times Union* newspaper article Reverend John Johnson, pastor of The First Church of God in Christ on Franklin Street, reminisced about black religious life in the South End in the 1930s. He said, "There wasn't much religious activity—Reverend Crenshaw [at the Union Baptist Church] on Franklin Street and Louis Parson and J. B. Holmes on Green Street were the only ones in the early '30s. There wasn't too many people around who seemed interested in doing anything."[92]

The explosion of storefront churches is considered one of the Great Migration's major religious consequences. A storefront

Table 3. Storefront Churches in Albany, New York, in 1928

Church of God and Saints of Christ—66 Dongan Avenue
Union Missionary Baptist Church—Grand Street near Herkimer Street
Independent Church of God and Souls of Christ—Franklin &
    Herkimer streets
The House of God (also known as, The Chuch of the Living God, the
    Ground and the Pillar of Truth)—88 Third Street
First Christ's Sanctified Church—94 Third Street
Third Street A.M.E. Chapel—Third Street
B.P.T. Church Gospel Mission—64 Herkimer Street
New Beulah Baptist—Herkimer Street

Source: National Urban League, Department of Research and Investigation, *The Negro Population—Albany, New York* (New York: National Urban League, 1928), 38.

church is a small congregation meeting in facilities not designed for worship or other religious gatherings, for example, an abandoned storefront, an apartment, or a house.[93] These types of churches are characteristically marginal to mainstream churches, lack theologically trained preachers, have a majority of female parishioners, and have an inclination toward Pentecostal ritual and Holiness doctrine.[94] Migrants trying to reorganize the congregations that had moved from the South occupied storefront churches in Albany. The storefront churches were popular among migrants because many of the old-line black churches in northern communities tended to adapt to the religious and political outlook of the upper classes and blacks who were race conscious. Historian Seth Scheiner summarizes this phenomenon.

> Among Negro Churches, even those of the same denomination, class division became more apparent as a city's black population increased. Lower-class blacks, on the one hand, found services at middle- and upper-class churches too restrained and the size

of the congregations too large and forbidding. On the other hand, many of the middle- and upper-class churches attempted to divorce themselves from what they considered the over emotionalism of the lower-class houses of worship. Through their places of worship, middle-class churchgoers often manifested their feelings of status and divorced themselves from the mass of blacks.[95]

The Morning Star Baptist Church was a local example of a middle- and upper-class black church that was affiliated with the M. C. Lawton Club, a race organization that sought to improve conditions for African Americans in Albany. Several of the M. C. Lawton Club's programs took place at the Morning Star Baptist Church, such as on 10 February 10 1928 when the Club commissioned the famous black poet Countee Cullen to read his poetry celebrating African American talent and culture.[96] Newly arrived migrants were looking for southern religious practices, not race politics and class structure.

One storefront church in Albany that met the needs of its southern congregation was the First Church of God in Christ (later called Wilborn Temple First Church of God in Christ.) This church was founded in 1927 when Charlotte Resper, a Buffalo, New York, missionary, came to Albany to conduct a revival at Union Missionary Baptist Church. The Wilborn Temple's seventy-fifth anniversary dedication book says of the 1927 revival, "The Revival reached beyond the walls of the church and found its way into the home of a member of the church, Ms. Elsie Black. Mrs. Alice Charles Harmon was drawn by the Spirit of God to the house where she surrendered to the will of God. These sisters banned together in prayer and supplication and in studying God's Word and fasting."[97] The outcome was a prayer circle.

The First Church of God in Christ was established when several preachers joined Resper, Black, and Harmon and established a new church in Albany. Among those who first preached at 40

Franklin Street in Albany's South End were Elder Lacy from Buffalo, Elder Richardson from Connecticut, and Elder Walker from New York City. But it was not until later in 1927 that Louis W. Parson moved from Shubuta, Mississippi, to Albany, New York, to become the first permanent pastor to the First Church of God in Christ's deeply devoted members.[98]

ELDER LOUIS W. PARSON

Elder Louis W. Parson, born in 1902, was a part-time preacher from Buckatunna, Mississippi. In addition to preaching at revivals throughout Mississippi, he also worked as a striker in the logging industry to support himself and his wife, Frances. Parson was injured while working on the job, so his company gave him a large cash settlement. (Orlean Rucker, Parson's niece, says that Parson worked for the railroad, while Labor Johnson, Parson's friend and peer said that Parson was a logger. Both however, confirm that Parson was injured on the job.) Not feeling comfortable with a large amount of money in Mississippi, Parson and his wife decided to leave and move north in 1927. Orlean Rucker recalled "No Negro was supposed to have a whole lot of money down there, so he left with his wife, Frances. They came, intending to go to Ohio, but he just wasn't rested there. He could not get himself acclimated to the area. So he said, 'Come on Frances let's go.' So they packed up and left and drove and drove. When they got to Albany they stopped because there were four ladies in a small church [conducting prayer meetings and trying to spread the word of God]."[99] It is not known if Parson knew the small congregation needed a full-time pastor prior to his arrival, but regardless Parson felt a kinship with the members of the prayer circle and joined the small congregation at 40 Franklin Street and the First Church of God in Christ was established. When Elder Parson was asked why he came to Albany, he always responded, "God led me to Albany."[100]

After the church was established, Parson traveled to Shubuta and the surrounding area to recruit members for his Albany congregation. He recruited his family, friends, and congregation members from the South because "He saw a greater promise for people to get an education and acquire jobs that were not picking cotton or digging in cornfields."[101] Sometimes it was difficult for sharecroppers to leave the South because of their supposed debts. One of Parson's recruitment tactics was to travel to Memphis, Tennessee, every November for the Church of God in Christ's convocation meetings, pick up people there, and return to Albany with them.[102] Parson also traveled directly to southern plantations. Just before Parson was expected, sharecroppers sold all their belongings and put their money together. He picked the sharecroppers up on Saturday nights, because on Sunday the landowners assumed they were at church all day. Parson loaded his car with as many people as he could. One time, it was claimed, he filled his Buick with seventeen people, and rations for them.[103] Large amounts of food were necessary because blacks were not allowed to patronize restaurants in the South. Orlean Rucker remembered people saying, "Oh! Elder Parson gonna take us to Memphis." From there they came to Albany.[104] Parson took different routes to and from the South. Some migrants remember traveling from Shubuta to Louisville, Kentucky, Cincinnati, Ohio, Cleveland, Ohio, where Parson's sister Abbey Steel lived, and then straight to Albany.[105] Parson's tactic to increase church size was different from other southern preachers. Most followed their congregations north. In 1917, one pastor from Ensley, Alabama, reported to his bishop after losing fifty-two of his ninety-six-member congregation, "I just come up here to notify you that I'm getting ready to follow my flock."[106]

Parson made several trips back and forth between Albany and Shubuta. Most of the people he brought to Albany settled in the South End and became members of his congregation. Caesar Moore was one of the first to come north with Parson. Chester and

Jerome Parson (Parson's brothers) came along on his second trip to Albany. Parson's third trip brought Ida Jones, Arment Young, and Jack (John) Johnson. His fourth trip in October 1933 brought Daniel McCann, Willie McCann, Sonny McCann, and members of the Johnson family. All of these migrants became charter members in Parson's church.[107]

Parson was not the only person to persuade family and friends in Mississippi to move to Albany. Clara Johnson, brought by Parson on his fourth trip, convinced Samuel and Luella Franklin to move to Albany by telling them that schools were so close to housing in Albany that you could easily walk to them. Johnson also sent the Franklin family clothing from the Salvation Army that she told them was located right around the corner from her house.[108] The persuasion worked because Parson brought the Franklin family to Albany in 1936.[109]

Parson brought so many blacks north that supposedly Albany authorities arrested him.[110] They did not want him bringing people to Albany who did not have money, jobs, or houses. He received an Albany Court summons, but it was during a time he was scheduled to go down to Mississippi. In an interview with Rucker, she remembered her uncle saying, "I don't have time for the judge."[111] Rucker also remembered, "He [Parson] was so committed to Jesus Christ and to God's people and for the betterment of our people, the black race. He told Frances [Parson's wife] she could go to court, but he had to go [down South]. . . . She said she was scared to death because she didn't know what to do, but knew she had to go to court because L. W. wasn't there, he told her to tell the judge whatever. She did go, she said she sat there and waited for the judge to call her up. But they never called her name, or his name. She was scared going home because she didn't know if they were gonna arrest [her] or something. Nobody ever heard anything after that."[112] Elder Parson continued bringing people to Albany until his death on 11 January 1940.

Parson influenced others to help in his quest to bring blacks to the North. He brought several members of the Johnson family on his trips to Albany from Shubuta. On one such trip Parson brought Jack Johnson. Johnson's son, McKinley Johnson, recalled his father's trip to Albany in the early 1930s.

> His [Johnson's] experience was that in the rural South in Shubuta, he accepted Christ in his life at the age of eighteen-nineteen years old. Because he was the youth leader in that community, even before he was converted, and the leader of the little local church in Shubuta, he was the leader when the itinerant preacher was not there. There was a gentleman named L. W. Parson, he was a pastor who was a planter of churches. He had a terrible accident on the railroad and received a large sum of money. With the large sum of money he came north and planted a church in Hartford, Connecticut, Staten Island, and a church in Albany. From what I understand he was steadily going south to bring up people.... He went down and picked up a number of people in the vicinity of Shubuta, not just Shubuta. Parson was the pastor of that church in Shubuta, my father being the youth leader, came with him with a number of other people. They went to Cleveland, Ohio, and picked up some additional people. Now if I understand correctly the limousine he had was like a three-seater. It had a front seat, a seat in the middle, and a seat in the back. By the time he got to Albany he was bringing sixteen people in the car, my father being one of them. He [Johnson] came to Albany with a few pair of pants, and a few shirts, and maybe a jacket. I don't know what season.[113]

Jack Johnson must have admired Parson, because when law officials started harassing Parson, Johnson began bringing people from the South.[114] Between 1937 and 1957, Johnson was responsible for "rescuing" one hundred blacks from the South and driving them to Albany.[115] Johnson was quoted once as saying, "I saw all that suffering, all that agony, so I said to myself that someday I'm going to do something about it.... One time I had twelve people in one car, but they had no choice if you wanted to get out of bondage."[116]

Johnson's tactics of "rescuing" blacks from the South were carefully thought out. He beeped his horn upon arrival into town. Later the same night, he would drive quietly onto a plantation and hoot softly, like a dove. The people quietly sneaked off the plantation into his waiting car or bus. Sometimes the 1,300-mile ride took two and a half days, "Old car, bad road . . . I wanted this long-suffering people to be lifted out of oppression."[117] McKinley Johnson remembered his father's trips to Mississippi. "He [Jack Johnson] would drive down there and before he left people would ask him, 'What time Brother Jack?' he would respond, 'When I blow my horn.' Most times it was two or three o'clock in the morning. He would blow the horn, they would have their bags packed and they would run out and get in the car. . . . The funny thing about it is he would drive all the way to Mississippi and get there that day and then leave that night. I always wondered why he did that. Didn't he need the rest? He always had to get back because he had to go to work and he had a family to provide for."[118]

Nora Lee McCann remembered her trip north with Elder Jack Johnson. "We had fourteen people in the car. We came up on Route 11 and we just tried to make it to the Mason-Dixon Line and I just wanted to see Albany, I just wanted to see the streets. I had twenty cents in my pocket. I bought ice cream for ten cents and had ten cents when I got here [Albany]. Elder Jack Johnson brought me here."[119] Emma Dickson stated that like Parson, Jack Johnson also upset law officials. Mississippi law officials supposedly put a bounty on Jack Johnson's head.[120]

Although Parson and Johnson brought many Mississippi families to Albany, many came on their own. Once a few families moved here, word of mouth spread between Albany, Shubuta, and all points south. The Woodard family lived in Hattiesburg, Mississippi, when they received word from family members Daniel and Willie McCann, who were both brought to Albany by Parson, that Albany was a land of opportunity. Girlie Ferguson, the oldest daughter of Alfred and Leola Woodard, recalled, in an interview, moving to Albany in 1939:

> When I was about eleven, almost twelve, my Uncle Dan and Uncle Willie, sometime in the late twenties or early thirties had moved to Albany. They sent for my grandmother and my grandfather. Wherever my grandfather and grandmother went, my mom and dad went, too. So we all packed up and got ready to come to Albany. We came by Greyhound bus; there were ten of us. There was my grandfather, Sam McCann, my grandmother, Nora McCann, my dad, Alfred Woodard, my mother, Leola Woodard, and my brother, Alfred, Jr., and my sister, Oseana, and my brother, Walter . . . and two cousins, Catherine and Mary. We boarded the Greyhound bus and of course all the neighbors and friends came to the bus station to see us off. It was just a big family reunion when we got ready to come. When we got to Albany, my Uncle Willie and Uncle Dan were there to pick us up at the bus station. My grandmother, grandfather, and two cousins, Mary and Catherine, lived with my Uncle Dan at 30 Dongan Avenue. My mother, my father, my brother Woody [Alfred, Jr.], my sister, Huttie [Oseana], and my brother, Sonny [Walter], lived with my Uncle Willie at 39 Dongan Avenue.[121]

Another South End family who traveled north and joined the First Church of God in Christ upon arrival in Albany were Sammie and Henrietta Fantroy. They moved to Albany shortly after their marriage in 1942. Henrietta Fantroy was originally from Pine Land, South Carolina, and Sammie Fantroy was originally from Evergreen, Alabama. The couple had an uncle who lived in Hudson, New York. They visited him for six months and then returned to South Carolina.[122] Upon returning to South Carolina, another uncle told the couple, "Y'all get back up in that North and stay there."[123] The couple returned north and have lived in Albany ever since. In an interview with the couple, Henrietta Fantroy recalled, "I didn't understand when I first got here, coming from a southern state, you can walk around houses, all the way around outside. When I got here everything was joined together. You could go out the back door, but you couldn't go around the houses. That was amusing to me."[124]

As the number of people Parson and Johnson brought to Albany increased, so did the congregation of the First Church of God in Christ. Throughout the 1930s the congregation moved to several different storefront locations, South Ferry Street, Green Street, and 23 Dongan Avenue.[125] In the late 1930s, the church found a permanent location at 79 Hamilton Street. The Wilborn Temple First Church of God in Christ's seventy-fifth anniversary book recorded the history of its increasing congregation: "Membership increased as more Albany residents came to the Lord. Elder Parson's door-to-door ministry and prayers drew hungry souls to Christ. The body was strengthened when former members of Elder Parson's church[es] in Mississippi migrated to the City of Albany. . . . Packed with parcels of clothing, bags of peanuts, vegetables and other necessities, he prepared for the long ride to Albany. Children were squeezed in between the adults. However, they all made it to the 'promised land.' "[126]

Upon their arrival, many of those aided in coming to Albany by Parson and Johnson settled in Albany's South End. These transplanted southerners found apartments on Green Street, Second Street, Dongan Avenue, Bleecker Street, Hamilton Street, Herkimer Street, Westerlo Street, Van Zandt Street, lower Madison Avenue, Fulton Street, and Franklin Street. In an interview, Girlie Ferguson remembered getting settled in her family's new apartment on 39 Dongan Avenue, the building they moved to upon their arrival in Albany.

> My mother did domestic work. She did work for a lady named Mrs. Condon [who lived on Hollywood Avenue off of New Scotland Avenue] . . . Mrs. Condon helped mom get things to-

gether to get her own place, like furniture. I remember my mom saying Mrs. Condon had an account at Montgomery Wards out in Menands. Mom went there and got certain things we needed on Mrs. Condon's account. I supposed Mrs. Condon deducted whatever payment from mom's salary. We didn't bring any furnishings with us, just clothing and things like that. We just came ourselves.[127]

After finding housing, many of the migrants who attended the First Church of God in Christ found employment. The most common employment for a black woman was domestic work, although there were a few exceptions. Elizabeth McCann owned and operated Doll's Beauty Salon from the early 1940s to the mid-1980s.[128] Tempie McCann worked at William's Press, and Leola Woodard worked at the Albany Arsenal.[129] Information from the Albany City directories shows that most of the men found "laborer" type employment. Again, there were exceptions. Willie McCann held a supervisory position at the Port of Albany.[130] Sammie Fantroy was a butcher at Tobin Packing Company.[131] Jessie Garrett worked at New York Power and Light. Erskine Nabors, Sr., worked as a machine operator at Allegheny Ludlum Steel.[132] Albany City directories indicate that many, although not all, of the men changed jobs frequently.

Similar to other northern churches that catered to southern migrants, the church that Parson created helped its members with several aspects of daily life. For example, Geneva Conway's family joined Parson's church upon arrival in Albany. Conway said, "Rental was not such a bad thing for my family, but it was not such a bad thing because we had the church that interceded for us and found housing for us."[133] Several migrants were able to find employment in Albany because fellow church members already had established contacts in Albany. The First Church of God in Christ also had a store during the 1930s to aid its members during the Depression. Lastly, Parson's church even went so far as to supply land for its members to buy and build houses on. This land is known as the Rapp Road community.

For many of the black families who attended the First Church of God in Christ, church was a major part of their daily lives. Members of the congregation attended services on Tuesday, Friday, and Sunday. The Church of God in Christ (COGIC) is a predominantly black Pentecostal church that was formed in 1897 by Bishop Charles Harrison Mason in Jackson, Mississippi. Originally, these churches were principally located in Tennessee, Arkansas, Mississippi, and Oklahoma, but today the church is the second largest black denomination and claims a worldwide membership of 8,000,000.[134] Core beliefs shared by COGIC members include the active manifestations of the Holy Spirit and spirit baptism, both evidenced through the phenomenon of speaking in tongues and mandatory for all members. Followers of this church also emphasize biblical literalism, conversion, and moral rigor.[135]

These beliefs caused some internal conflicts for the newly settled people from the South. The environment in the South End made some of these people unhappy. During the first half of the twentieth century, several gambling houses, bars, and prostitutes occupied the South End area. According to William Kennedy, "Dongan Avenue had had for some years the reputation of being one of the lifelines of the red-light district. It was such a lowly street that in 1965 the city did not even collect its garbage."[136] For some time the First Church of God in Christ and many of its members resided on Dongan Avenue. Furthermore, according to Reverend John (Jack) Johnson of St. John's Church of God in Christ, "His recollection of the South End Negro social life of those early days was that it centered around 'small clubs and a few taverns—that's where you would see most of the people hanging around.' "[137] Charlie Van Buren remembered that one of the first black nightclubs in Albany was on the corner of Division Street and Dongan Avenue. It was run by a man named Piano Nelson with Boo Tucker working there as the club's singer.[138] As a result, several of these churchgoing families did not want to raise their children in this neighborhood. Secondly, most of the people who were brought to Albany had been sharecroppers in the South. They were used to a rural environment of working the land, raising animals, and building what they needed. Going to the store to buy everything was probably a new concept for most. Some decided to move back South after living in the South End for a short while. Girlie Ferguson remembered, "My grandfather didn't like Albany, so he went back South. My grandmother stayed and she eventually came to live with my mom and dad."[139]

Elder Parson gave his congregation much more than church service on Sunday. The church became the place where its members could somewhat continue their southern lifestyle while in the North. Albany was the land of opportunity for many African American migrants, but only to a degree. Discrimination kept many black families from proper housing, good jobs, and equal opportunities in education. Geneva Conway recalled, "My mother said in the South I knew segregation for what it was, but in the North you are sneaky about it. Down there I knew what I had to face. Now that I have come north it just kind of sneaks its way in and you are on me before I know it."[140] When Elder Parson realized that members of his congregation were unhappy with the living conditions in the South End, he set out to remedy the situation.

CHAPTER 3

"Whatever We Needed, He Could Get It"

There was a consensus among Parson's congregation that "Whatever we needed he could get it."[1] This statement was true on many levels. Parson provided for his people. Not only did he supply them with the transportation out of a harsh southern life, but he also supplied them with housing, employment, and religious guidance upon their arrival in the North. Northern city life was difficult for some members of Parson's congregation. Many of these deeply religious people did not like living in close proximity to bars, prostitution, and gambling. Parson decided to provide an alternative to city life for his congregation. The result was the Rapp Road community (see appendix 8).

ESTABLISHMENT OF THE RAPP ROAD COMMUNITY

Louis Parson realized that members of his congregation were unhappy with the living situation in the South End. He set out to remedy the situation. On 2 May 1930, Parson and William Toliver

Part of chapter 3 was originally published in an article entitled "Albany and the Great Migration," in *Afro-Americans in New York Life and History* (January 2008): Vol. 32, No. 1, January 2008, pp. 47–68.

purchased a fourteen-acre tract of land from Charles Smith.[2] On 30 March 1933, Parson and his wife, Frances, purchased another fourteen-acre tract of land from Smith.[3] Each tract of land cost $400 and was paid for in quarterly installments of $50 with an interest rate of 6 percent per annum.[4] This land was located in the western extension of the city of Albany in an area known as the Pine Bush. The acreage Parson and Toliver purchased was rural, surrounded only by a few farms. Parson's plan was to only sell tracts of land to members of his congregation so they could get away from city life.[5] It is possible that they allowed the members of the congregation to begin clearing their land and building homes before the transfer of land was official. The Toliver family was the first to build on Rapp Road and invited the Parsons to move in with them. Parson's niece, Orlean Rucker, recalled that one of the land buyers told her, "Oh, I was so happy when your uncle bought that land and sold me a piece of it. I bought two acres of land for $90."[6] Assistant Pastor of Wilborn Temple Willie McCann remembered buying his wooded land for $90 cash in 1945[7] (see appendix 9).

Before families could move to Rapp Road, the land had to be cleared and houses built. At this point in time, blacks were not awarded mortgages. Each family had to build their house on a "pay as you go system," and as a result most of the families built their own homes with the help of neighbors and other family members. Rapp Road residents incorporated many of the same architectural elements used in their southern homes, except that many of the Rapp Road homes had basements; their southern counterparts were up on stilts because of constant flooding.

Many of the residents on Rapp Road stayed in their Albany city apartments until their houses were at least partially built. Ralph McCann recalled moving into his family's new house on 38 Rapp Road in the mid-1940s. "We lived in the South End until our house was livable, but it wasn't really livable. When we first moved here, you could look right through the walls, it was just the structure.... The structure in the basement, the beams, came from the out in back [the backyard]. My father [Daniel McCann] used to cut down the trees, took the trees to the mill, and brought them back here.... When we first came out here my father dug a well for water."[8]

Juanita Nabors's parents, Willie and Tempie McCann, moved to Rapp Road in 1945. Nabors recalled, "We lived in the South End while my father was building the house. The kitchen was completed and the bathroom was completed. Everything else was not completed. Everything was built by hand. He [Willie McCann] not only built this house [at 23 Rapp Road], but he built Javan Owens's house [at 5 Rapp Road], he had a hand in the Woodards' house [at 22 Rapp Road], he help build Dan McCann's house [38 Rapp Road], he built the house at 29 [Rapp Road]. My father was a carpenter by trade, but it was just a pastime for him."[9]

Caesar Moore, an original member of the First Church of God in Christ, bought large tracts of land on Rapp Road from Parson and eventually subdivided and also sold them to church members. The land that he owned was on the south end of Rapp Road near the Pine Lane intersection. Some of the earliest houses built on Rapp Road used whatever materials could be found. Both Caesar Moore's and Albert Farley's homes were made from crates and cardboard. These houses were eventually replaced with more permanent structures.[10]

When Alfred and Leola Woodard and their children moved to Rapp Road, they did things a bit differently. Girlie Ferguson, oldest of the Woodard children, reminisced about the building of her family's house.

In late 1944, my mom and dad started building their house out on Rapp Road. My mom worked for Watervliet Arsenal, and they would buy materials to build the house as they got the money enough to buy. It seemed that there were timbers or something that they needed, but because it was the wartime it was hard to get certain materials. So they had certain things lying around, like some lumber that you wouldn't put in a house. So my mom said to my dad, "Let's build a shotgun house. And we'll live in the shotgun house. That way we can save money to buy materials." At that time they [the Woodards] were living on Market Street and of course they had to pay utilities and such. . . . My dad said, "No, I'm building the new house." My Uncle Dan and Uncle Willie were living out there already, and they helped my dad lay the bricks or concrete blocks. That's how they got the big house started. Then my mom said, "Okay, I'm gonna build the shotgun house," or the little house, that's what we called it. And she started building it . . . and then she started to get so far ahead on the little house that dad stopped building on the new house and started helping her. And that's where ma and dad and my brothers and sisters were living when Emma, my sister, was born. My mom did everything my grandfather and her brothers did. . . . They lived in the little house until 1949. At that point the big house was livable. February of 1949, my mom and dad and siblings moved into the big house.[11]

Eventually, the little house was torn down and the big house remains in the family.

Parson died on 11 January 1940, before all the tracts were sold. After the death of her first husband, Frances Parson married William Wilborn in 1942.[12] Wilborn and Parson met when Parson recruited members for his new church. He went door to door asking people to attend the service. Orlean Rucker recalled the first meeting between Parson and Wilborn.

My uncle [Parson] went knocking on doors asking people to attend his service. He went to the Wilborn house on Green Street. I'd never forget that. He told him [Wilborn] to come out and he said he wasn't interested in the church. He bought his supply of beer, supply of liquor, and supply of cigars and that's what he was going to do all week. But my uncle was so impressed with him [Wilborn] that they went to the church that night, and he got saved that night! And he went home and threw out all his liquor and cigars and beer and everything. He [Wilborn] was a monumental force within our church. He became a minister and then my uncle [Parson] decided he should become a district official from Albany down to Nyack, New York. He stayed with the church.[13]

After Parson's death, Wilborn became the pastor of the First Church of God in Christ. Under Wilborn's leadership, the debt from buying the building on 79 Hamilton Street was paid and it was subsequently remodeled to accommodate the growing congregation.[14] In 1949 the church was incorporated as the First Church of God in Christ, Inc. Years later, the Albany church was renamed, Wilborn Temple First Church of God in Christ, in honor of Wilborn. In February 1967 Wilborn was consecrated bishop. He was the first black bishop to preside in Upstate New York.[15]

Frances Parson Wilborn continued to make her first husband's hopes and plans a reality. She continued to sell the Pine Bush land to members of the congregation. The names Frances Parson and Frances Wilborn both appear on the original list of land deeds. Officially, between 1942 and 1963 twenty-three families bought tracts from Parson's and Toliver's original land purchases. The Rapp Road community was family oriented. McKinley Johnson remembered why his father, John "Jack" Johnson, did not move there. "My father had a piece of property out there in the beginning. But mostly families were out there and he was single. He wasn't married for a few years after coming here, and so he [lived in the city.]"[16] Only members of the First Church of God in Christ were offered this land. The road that traversed this area was named Rapp Road after the Rapp family that had lived and farmed the area for decades[17] (see appendix 10).

LIFE ON RAPP ROAD

Most of the people who moved from the South were farmers. One of the reasons many did not like city life was because they had to go to the store for everything. Once families moved to Rapp Road, they began growing crops and raising animals. Many of the families were practically self-sufficient. They had livestock, including pigs, chickens, cows, goats, and turkeys. Many of the men hunted for wild game. Because land was abundant on Rapp Road, families had fields of vegetables, not gardens. Families grew corn, cucumbers, collard greens, potatoes, tomatoes, and many other vegetables. Emma Dickson recalled her mother and aunts canning food in the summer. "I remember my mother and my aunts spending long summer days in the kitchen, and there would be huge pots on the stove with boiling jars, canning jars, and they would put food in them. When people had no pears, or whatever, you could go into my parents' basement and there were shelves and shelves from the floor to the ceiling and they were filled with jelly, pickles, tomatoes, fruits, [and] vegetables. The things that I [now] go to the store to buy were in my mother's basement. . . . They had to buy flour and sugar from the store. We had a dairy cow, so I knew how to churn milk and gather butter."[18]

Daniel McCann raised pigs, chickens, and cows. He had a hundred pigs until the city of Albany rezoned the area as residential, and he therefore was not allowed to have any farm animals. He bought property outside of the city and raised the pigs there.[19] McCann also had a workhorse for plowing.

Although many of the original landowners on Rapp Road were farmers, some were not. When Sammie Fantroy got out of the service in 1946 he bought land on Rapp Road from Caesar Moore. The Fantroy's began building their house in 1949. Sammie Fantroy worked at Tobin Packing Company, and he chose to have a small garden instead of big fields and livestock[20] (see appendix 11).

The residents on Rapp Road all worshiped in the same church, moved to Albany from the same part of the country, had similar upbringings, and settled on Rapp Road around the same time. As a result, the community on Rapp Road was a tight-knit one. Emma Dickson recalled, "Everyone out on Rapp Road did everything together. You took care of each other's children. They went to church together, they had prayer meetings together. Whatever had to be done, you got together and did it."[21] One example of this community unity occurred when the city of Albany would not provide a school bus for the Rapp Road children. The city officials claimed the roads near Rapp Road were too narrow for the bus to travel. Elder Wilborn, the people in the church, and the Rapp Road community got together and bought a school bus.[22] Rapp Road resident Leola Woodard was the bus driver, the first black female bus driver in Albany.

Growing up on Rapp Road during the 1950s and 1960s was different from what most children in Albany experienced, mainly because it was a church community. Emma Dickson remembers that anything you did that was not congruent with church expectations resulted in a neighbor or family member stepping in and making sure you did the right thing. Dickson recalled, "My uncle once caught me with fingernail polish on. He said, 'You know you're not supposed to have that jezebel fingernail polish on.'"[23] Another example of what it was like to live in a close-knit church community was when Dickson and her sisters were allowed to go their Aunt Doll's (Elizabeth McCann's) beauty shop on Dongan Avenue to get their hair done for church. Dickson fondly recalled the following incident.

> She [Aunt Doll McCann] would say, "Bring the girls down and I'll do their hair for church." So we would go to her shop. Her shop was on Dongan Avenue and it was a basement shop, you went down a couple of stairs into a basement on Dongan Avenue. She was right in what they called the red-light district then. All

these women came in that my sister Ann and I thought were the most gorgeous women in the world. They would have their hair done up in all these wonderful up-do's and all this wonderful make-up on and we just thought they were the most beautiful women—not realizing that they were actually prostitutes, or as my Aunt Doll called them, women of the night. When they came into her shop they knew she belonged to the Pentecostal First Church of God in Christ and they knew that she was also a missionary. So when they came into the shop they knew they were not to talk any street business in her shop. When they would start talking to each other and whispering to each other, my sister Ann and I would try to get as close to them as we could so we could hear what they were saying. But before we could hear anything, my aunt would spy [on] them and tell them not to talk about such things in her shop! So we would want them to always keep talking, but she made them be quiet. So going to the city was a big deal for us.[24]

Dickson also remembers that growing up was fun. "There was no fear that anything could happen to you. Everyone who came down this road was one of the families that lived on this road. You could go up, down the road anywhere you wanted to. When we went to my cousin's house in the city, it was very different because we had to stay right in front of their house ... [On Rapp Road] I could run over to my uncle's house or run over to my aunt's house. When we first were out here, we didn't have telephones, [parents] could just yell out the window to tell you to come home."[25] Ralph McCann also remembered he had fun growing up on Rapp Road. He said he "played outside all day, but because it was so dark outside at night he always came inside then."[26]

McKinley Johnson, pastor of St. John's Church of God in Christ, located in Albany's South End, had several relatives on Rapp Road when he was young. In an interview Johnson recalled what it was like to visit Rapp Road from his home in the South End.

When I was coming up as a youngster that [Rapp Road] was the place to go. A lot of my relatives lived out there. And it was always like country, not asphalt, not sidewalks, not city dwelling. When we said, "let's go to the country," we only meant Rapp Road. The country to us implied we went where we could run and jump and play and [had] plenty to eat and land and it's not streets. Not a lot of street lights. We were back home in Shubuta. [We were] back in the country, it was always a joy or a pleasure trip if we ever went to the country because we would visit Uncle Dan [McCann], Aunt Leola's [Woodard] . . . It was country, it was the South, it was Shubuta, and it was home. Only blacks lived there.[27]

Johnson, similar to the Rapp Road children, remembered that most of his experiences while growing up came from the church. The Johnson family celebrated Easter by attending church and going to Rapp Road for an Easter egg hunt.[28]

The children on Rapp Road attended School 27 for their elementary education. During the 1940s through the 1960s, they were basically the only black children at that school. For junior high, the children attended W. S. Hackett, and then Albany High School. Emma Dickson said some of the children felt that it was an adventure to go into the city of Albany, because it was so different from Rapp Road. Dickson, her sister, Ann, and their cousin, Ralph McCann, had one such adventure in the city of Albany. One Sunday after church Ralph's older brother, Robert, gave them some money to go to the movie theater despite the church policy prohibiting children from watching certain movies because they were considered "other worldly."[29] The three children decided to go to the Palace Theater to see their first movie. Dickson reminisced about the event.

One of our friends from school was there, so she showed us how to go to the window and buy a ticket. So the three of us go into the movies and we go upstairs and sit down. So the movie screen is just coming on and the first pictures are starting to show and everyone in the whole theater just started screaming at the top of their lungs. Ralph, my sister, and I decided we had done something so terrible that the movie had been struck by lightening and God must have struck down and the movie must be on fire or something. So we jump up out of our chairs, ran downstairs out of the movie theater as fast as we could. We ran into the girl that helped us and we told her the movie was on fire. She said the movie was not on fire and that everyone was screaming because Elvis Presley came on the screen and had started to sing. We did not stay because at our church if you did these worldly things it meant Hell brimstone and fire, so we left flying out of the theater right into Brother Artis Kitchen who was on his way back to church waiting for a bus in front of the Palace Theater. . . . We told him we were waiting for the bus to church too. But when we came out of the theater, you could smoke in the theater then, we had to start fanning our coats because we knew when we went back to church our clothes were going to smell like smoke. We were terrified, but thankfully our parents never found out we snuck off that day.[30]

Since they lived in such a tight-knit community, many of the Rapp Road children did not face racial discriminations until they left the community. Dickson recalled an incident when she was first married. "I went to look at an apartment on Ten Broeck Place [in downtown Albany] . . . the landlord said I could only look at apartments on a certain side of the building. . . . He said, 'most of the black people live on this side of the building.' Coming from Rapp Road, I said, 'well I'm not most of the black people, I want to know why and how you can do that?' "[31]

Until the 1980s, Albany politics seemed to have left Rapp Road alone. Most of the residents usually voted Democrat. Politicians rarely came out to Rapp Road to garner votes. Javan Owens was the principal Rapp Road resident who dealt with politicians. He took petitions around the neighborhood and told people about the candidates. Ward leaders did not appear on Rapp Road until

Mayor Erastus Corning, 2nd, stepped in. In the early 1980s, the city of Albany ran a candidate who was not familiar with the Rapp Road community. Emma Dickson refused to sign the candidate's petition, and then she called her ward leader. The ward leader did not return her calls so Dickson decided to call Mayor Erastus Corning, 2nd. Corning spoke with Dickson directly, assuring her that her ward leader would be calling. Dickson recalled, "Well, after that not only did my ward leader call me, my ward leader appeared in my driveway the next day. When I came home from work his big Lincoln was sitting in my driveway. He seemed very annoyed with me that I called the mayor's office. He wanted to know why I wouldn't sign the petition for this person. And I told him why, and then he said, 'If you think you can do a better job, then you run.' I said, 'Thank you, I will.' "[32] Dickson soon became a committee chairperson, a title she holds until the present time. After this incident the Rapp Road residents received quick responses from their city leaders.

The majority of the first-generation Rapp Road residents lived there until their deaths. The oldest Rapp Road residents were buried in Graceland Cemetery located in southern Albany, while later settlers, or those first-generation settlers that lived a long time, were buried in Evergreen Cemetery in Schenectady, New York.

THE FIRST CHURCH OF GOD IN CHRIST AND THE RAPP ROAD COMMUNITY

The Rapp Road community was, and still is, deeply devoted to its church. The First Church of God in Christ held daily twelve o'clock services. Often the women on Rapp Road who did not go to work during the day did not have transportation to the city for noon church service. These women formed a prayer group and took turns hosting noonday prayers in their homes.[33] They usually met at the Toliver house (8 Rapp Road), the Moore house (71 Rapp Road), or the Burney house (unknown number Rapp Road.)[34] Emma Dickson remembers going to these prayer groups as a child.

> I was one of the youngest children in the community because I was born in 1944 when my parents moved out here. So therefore my whole life as a young adult was on Rapp Road and so it involved church and school. My siblings are a lot older than me, we had eight in the family and I am the youngest. So when they were going to school, I was still at home and staying with my Aunt Tempie who lived across the street (23 Rapp Road) because my mother was going out and doing domestic work. So when I stayed with her I was home with the women who went to the prayer groups. At noonday my Aunt Tempie would pack up my lunch and get her straw hat and get her long stick and either start up the road toward Western Avenue or we would go in the opposite direction in the direction of where Washington Avenue Extension is now. That would take us to where Libbie Toliver's house was or where the Burney house was. My aunt would get this long stick, and I never knew what it was for until one day we met this snake in the road. She just took the stick and put it under the snake and just flip it up out of the road and just kept right on walking to her prayer meeting. That just shows you how determined they were to get to prayer meetings. I would have just probably turned around and went home. So as a child I would get a stick to go walking to prayer meetings also, just in case we met up with another snake. As a small child my whole world revolved around church.[35]

The community's devotion to their church was shown in ways other than worship. This was apparent when urban renewal resulted in the need for a new church. In the 1960s, forty square blocks of downtown Albany were demolished for the South Mall project. With it went 79 Hamilton Street, the First Church of God in Christ. Elder Wilborn was an instrumental force in acquiring the new church on 121 Jay Street, the site of the former

Temple Beth Emeth synagogue. The congregation was not able to get a mortgage from a local bank, but eventually found a bank in Syracuse, New York, that gave them one.[36] Wilborn Temple members came together and put up money for the new church. Orlean Rucker remembered her mother and father donating money for the new church. "I remember my mother told my father, 'Johnny we gotta give that money, because Brother Wilborn has got a place where we're gonna move.' He said, 'Luella, I'm saving money to buy a house.' My mother was so insistent. 'Never mind the house. We gotta have a church.' So eventually my daddy gave her the money because he loved her so much."[37] In addition to donations to purchase the new church, two members of the congregation listed their homes on Rapp Road as collateral. Willie McCann and William Wilborn were the two faithful people.[38] The church's seventy-fifth anniversary book stated, "Through prayer, fasting, sacrifice, labor, and the united effort of all members of the congregation, the mortgage ceremony took place in three years and ten months of a five-year contract."[39] On Sunday 8 September 1957, Wilborn Temple's congregation walked from their old church at 79 Hamilton to their new church at 121 Jay Street. The event was celebrated with prayer, music, and home cooked ham, turkey, and chicken dinners.[40] The location at 121 Jay Street continues to serve as the site of the Wilborn Temple First Church of God in Christ.

Despite the fact that the Rapp Road community was quite a distance (approximately seven miles) from the structures on 79 Hamilton and 121 Jay Street, many residents were involved with the church's activities and groups. Some of these groups included the Progressive Youth Choir, Senior Choir, the Electrifying Kitchenairs Choir, Pastor's Aid Board, Senior Usher Board, Junior Usher Board, Missionary Board, Mothers' Board, and the Hospitality Board. For example, Rapp Road residents Tempie McCann served on the Missionary Board and the Mothers' Board, Elizabeth McCann served as a Hospitality President, Carrie Burney was the first and only Assistant Church Mother, Caesar Moore was the Sunday School Superintendent between 1928 and 1963, Henrietta Fantroy served as a District Missionary, Sammie Fantroy served on the Deacon Board, and Willie McCann was a cochair of the Church of God in Christ International Women's Convention in 1964.[41]

Emma Dickson remembers being a member of the church's youth group that traveled to other COGIC congregations along the Hudson River. Dickson said the young people liked the traveling and that the church really tried to make sure there were activities for young people.[42] She also claimed that all the children on Rapp Road were involved with church activities. "All the kids on this road, we usually all got together and walked up to Western Avenue and got the bus to go to choir rehearsal or Junior Usher Board practice."[43]

The central social roll played by the church has changed little from the settlement of the community to present day. The church remains at the center of the community and it continues to serve as a conservator of the cultural and social values of the past. Yet, third- and fourth-generation Rapp Road residents and younger Wilborn Temple members do not adhere to the strict attendance rules that their elders once did. The Tuesday and Friday noonday prayer services and Sunday, Tuesday, and Friday evening worship services are usually not attended by many of the younger congregants because of busy family and work schedules.[44] Younger generations learn about the church and its traditions during the Friday evening youth service and Sunday school instruction. Sunday morning services continue to be attended by most.

RAPP ROAD REUNION

As a strong sense of community began to develop the Rapp Road residents felt the need to celebrate. Looking to their southern experiences, they decided to hold a yearly reunion for family and friends. The idea of a reunion stems from homecoming, a southern reunion celebration that occurred in the late summer work lull because those who planted vegetables and fattened pigs enjoyed the bounty of their efforts.[45] Historian Peter Gottlieb wrote, "The July-August rest and celebration period was also a time for visiting relatives and friends. As the time passed and the numbers of southern migrants to northern cities grew, the late summer holiday became as closely associated with 'homecoming' as it was with church revivals. The break from field work provided an opportunity for those who had left to come back and visit, renewing old associations, while those who had remained on farms visited friends living in the surrounding area."[46]

Rapp Road residents looked to their own southern experiences to find an example of a homecoming celebration to copy. Often residents of Rapp Road and members of Wilborn Temple traveled to Shubuta for this biannual event. Shubuta resident Alma MacDonald recalled the homecomings that still occur there every two years. "My cousin wanted for everyone to come back to Shubuta to see what it looked like, so he started this homecoming. It starts on Friday. They have a picnic and a dance on Friday. On Saturday they cook fish and have a fish fry, people from all over the USA come. Then on Sunday they go to church."[47]

The Rapp Road reunion began in 1957 by Alfred and Leola McCann Woodard, Daniel McCann, and Willie McCann when one of their relatives from Buffalo, New York, was visiting Albany. Emma Dickson remembered the first Rapp Road reunion: "My mother made salads, someone else made another one of their recipes, so then my Uncle Dan [McCann] decided he was going to kill this pig and roast it."[48] Since this first reunion, the celebration continues to grow and grow. In fact, Daniel McCann built a small smokehouse on his property at 38 Rapp Road specifically for roasting pig at family reunions. The reunions originally took place on the third Sunday of September, but since children from out of town were missing school, the families decided to hold the reunion the third Sunday of August. Today, more than two hundred family members and friends come from all over the country. Rapp Road is blocked off, so kids play games, family members visit, and everyone enjoys a meal. To continue the tradition, the third- and fourth-generation Rapp Road members are taking over the reunion's organization so they can learn how it is done.[49]

RECREATION OF A SOUTHERN COMMUNITY

Louis W. Parson set out to recreate the rural southern life that many of his church members missed upon moving to Albany, New York. Parson did just that. The Rapp Road community's architecture, landscape, agriculture, and social customs are all similar to Shubuta, Mississippi's rural southern agricultural life (see appendix 12).

The landscape of Shubuta and Rapp Road are remarkably similar. Shubuta has an abundance of tall pine trees and a top layer of sandy soil because the area is located on the riverbanks of the Chickasawhay River. The Rapp Road community is located in an area known as the Pine Bush, which is a unique inland pitch pine scrub oak barrens with a sandy soil created from glaciers 15,000 years ago.[50]

Since the majority of Rapp Road residents were sharecropping farmers in Shubuta, they brought their southern agricultural practices with them. The Pine Bush offered these migrants an opportunity to, once again, cultivate land and grow produce, but now it would be for themselves, not a landowner. Community members cultivated large plots of land on Rapp Road. In both Shubuta and Albany farmers grew corn, sweet potatoes, cucumbers, collard greens, tomatoes, and watermelons. Also similar to their southern way of life Rapp Road residents raised livestock including pigs, chickens, cows, goats, and turkeys. Food preservation techniques such as canning and curing meats were learned in the South and passed down to the next generation living on Rapp Road.[51]

Social and religious customs were also passed between Mississippi and New York. The practice of full immersion baptisms in a river or creek was common in black churches in Shubuta and throughout rural Mississippi. The Wilborn Temple continued this tradition by baptizing in the Hudson River on the shallow Rensselaer side (east side) until the spring of 1957 when the city of Rensselaer banned the practice for safety reasons. As a result, Rapp Road resident Willie McCann built a baptism pool that is still used in church baptisms.[52] As noted earlier, the Rapp Road reunion was another social custom that migrants brought to Albany.

Rapp Road pioneers also brought their building techniques north. Being on the outskirts of the city of Albany, with no regular modes of transportation at their disposal, and with limited incomes, these migrants approached home building from a pragmatic and frugal standpoint. They built using available materials and drew upon their southern lifestyle and heritage as they made plans to build homes. Architecturally they brought both styles and methods with them from Mississippi. This makes all the more sense when comparing the topography of Shubuta with that of the Pine Bush in Albany.

The first shelters on Rapp Road were built in the "shotgun" style, a folk architecture closely associated with the rural South. This type of housing was used as worker's and tenant's housing dating from the nineteenth century when it is believed to have been brought to the United States by free blacks migrating from Haiti to Louisiana and Mississippi.[53] By the 1920s, it could be found throughout the country, especially in California, Chicago, and Rapp Road in Albany.

A shotgun house typically is one room wide with one to three all-purpose rooms following in succession. Entry to the structure is through a gable end. The name "shotgun" comes from the belief that if a gun was fired from the front of the structure, the pellets would pass through the entire length of the structure, never hitting a wall, and exiting out the rear. Both 29 and 53 Rapp Road are examples of shotgun houses that were eventually added on to. At 22 Rapp Road a small shotgun house was built to provide temporary shelter while permanent accommodations were being planned and built; the structure was eventually torn down. An example of this type of temporary housing can be found behind 23 Rapp Road, which is currently being used as a garage and shed.

Although these residents primarily drew upon southern, rural folk tradition styles in the design of their houses, they were also influenced by the dominant style sweeping small house construction throughout the United States from 1905 to the mid-1930s, the Craftsman-style bungalow. Vernacular examples of the Craftsman (and Prairie) style gained widespread distribution through popular magazines and pattern books. A home could be purchased, plans, parts, and all for as little as $1,000. It is easy to imagine the Rapp Road pioneers going up Western Avenue on their way home from a long day of work. They would pass some of Albany's most recently constructed neighborhoods (in the area between the current University at Albany campus and Stuyvesant Plaza.) The homes along Western Avenue and on side streets such as Waverly Place, McKown Road, Norwood, Glenwood, Parkwood, and Elmwood streets were developed after World War I until the years immediately before the Rapp Road community was settled. Most of these homes were built in the bungalow style. With this inspiration, and building plans readily available from a number of sources, Rapp Road builders incorporated features of this popular style into their new homes.

In looking at 5 Rapp Road, 8 Rapp Road, 14 Rapp Road, 39 Rapp Road, 59 Rapp Road, and 68 Rapp Road one can see the blending of southern rural traditions with bungalow stylistic detailing. The majority of the original post-shotgun Rapp Road houses were built in one- and two-story pyramidal family form. In the early decades of the twentieth century, this style became a popular replacement for the smaller hall-and-parlor houses throughout the South.[54] This type of construction, along with earlier French colonial forms, were the norm for new house building throughout the Shubuta area in the era that Rapp Road residents migrated north. In the Rapp Road pyramidal homes, the earlier French colonial influences, such as hipped roofs (some dual-pitched) with porches and dormers were also incorporated into the construction. One example of this is 67 Rapp Road. Later on open porches were enclosed to create more all-weather space, and second-floor living additions with the use of dormers provided new space for growing families. These same kinds of improvements and additions can be seen on comparable structures in the South. In fact, when viewing pictures of structures of Rapp Road and Shubuta side-by-side, it is difficult to determine which structures are located in the North or in the South.

It is not known why Louis Parson chose Albany as a place to settle and recruit his congregants north. This migration is unlike other examples that occurred during the Great Migration because it is difficult to travel from Shubuta to Albany. Most migrations during this time followed a direct north-south route because railroad lines ran in that direction. Chicago was a major destination for African American Mississippi migrants because it was directly north.[55] Conversely, the majority of Albany's southern migrants in 1920 and 1930 were from points directly south— Virginia, Georgia, North Carolina, and South Carolina.[56] Wilborn Temple church members and Rapp Road residents believe that God led Parson to Albany. This reasoning could explain how Parson was able to find an area of rural land within Albany City limits that looked identical to his southern home and, being an African American in a somewhat discriminatory social climate, actually have the wherewithal to buy the land and sell it to his homesick church members.

Whether through divine intervention or coincidence, the Rapp Road residents were able to buy homes, raise their own food, raise families, attend church, and basically live in an environment free of racism. The community continued to prosper and was so strong that it was able to withstand the commercial development of Albany's population flight to suburbia.

CHAPTER 4

Change Comes to Rapp Road

The Rapp Road community was left alone and undiscovered until Albany's population began moving out of downtown. Similar to many other older American cities by the middle of the twentieth century, Albany's downtown was dilapidated and in desperate need of repair. As a result, Albany's middle-class residents, once downtown dwellers, began moving westward to the Pine Bush and to the Albany suburbs of Guilderland and Colonie. For many, movement away from downtown was motivated by the pursuit of better quality of life, reduced air pollution, space for parking, and less traffic.[1]

In 1955, Albany's city government devised the South End Project to help alleviate the blighted downtown area. The South End Project was a federally funded urban renewal initiative designed to clear away old and abandoned buildings, improve the condition and size of downtown streets, provide parking garages for commuter traffic, and construct a modern hotel and shopping center downtown.[2] This plan, developed by Albany Mayor Erastus Corning, 2nd, was to be the largest urban renewal project in Albany since World War I. The South End Project never materialized. Three years after the city introduced the project nothing in the South End had been touched.[3] The project had too many problems that city administrators could not solve. Eventually, Corning abandoned the failed project. As a result, Albany administrators shifted their focus away from the blighted city core and looked to the Pine Bush for salvation.[4]

The first major development to affect the Pine Bush near the Rapp Road community was the building of the New York State Thruway in 1954. This 641-mile superhighway connects New York City and Buffalo, the state's two largest cities, and runs through Albany. Although not visible because of the tall pine trees characteristic of the area, the thruway runs a quarter mile north of the community. The *Times Union* (Albany) newspaper reported some of the first plans for the New York State Thruway in 1950 in an article titled "Wilderness within a City, Thruway May Reopen Pine Bush, Forbidden Wasteland within a Few Miles of Albany and Schenectady May Be Opened to Development by New Highway." Written before the time of environmentalism, the article had a depressing description of the Pine Barrens. "The Thruway will bisect the Pine Bush, but its traffic will be express. Beyond the point where Washington Avenue will join it as an arterial street, there will be no entrances or exits through this wasteland. Nevertheless, the Thruway may have an influence on opening the desolate tract to civilization, and perhaps even to real estate development. Cross-trails that are now barely passable to a car will be dignified with viaducts, and there improvement into real highways is foreseen."[5] Although the thruway did not directly affect the Rapp Road community, it was the first step toward commercial development near the rural area (see appendix 13).

The 1950 thruway newspaper piece was probably the first article to acknowledge the Rapp Road community's existence. The article stated, "The only residential development that has actually transpired is the community of colored people along Rapp Road . . .

> in the heart of the Bush. It now numbers 14 families, all members of the Pentecostal Church of God in Christ, on Hamilton Street in Albany.

Founder of the community was William Toliver, an ex-minister, who had a hankering to "get a place in the country." Back around 1930, at the age of 22, he was living in town and not liking it. A fellow workman on a truck told him about a hunk of land for sale in the Pine Bush. He and a friend, Louis Parsons, went out and looked it over, and purchased 28 acres. Toliver and his wife put up a small shack, and Parsons boarded with them. They made a little garden, raised a few pigs. After four years alone, they were joined by neighbors. One by one, the Tolivers sold a parcel of land to another colored family that wanted to get into the country.

Most of these people work in town. At home, they do a bit of farming, grow corn, keep some cows, pigs, chickens, and horses. The city plows the road in the winter. Neatest house in the un-named settlement is that of William Wilbur [Wilborn], awesomely tall Pentecostal clergyman who is pastor of the flock. In summer, they hold "Bible Band" meetings around at the homes.

Toliver admits that one idea he had in mind, besides living in the country, was to find a place where colored folk might be by themselves. He says the land he bought is all taken up now, and it's hard to get more.[6]

Although oral history interviews tell slight variations of the Rapp Road community's history, the author of the article captured several of the major points. Many Albany newspaper articles published during the Pine Bush development never mentioned anyone living in the Pine Bush other than squatters.[7]

In 1957 Albany Mayor Erastus Corning, 2nd announced his plans to create a complete community from scratch in the Pine Bush.[8] Shortly after, the Common Council approved a $27,500 appropriation for preliminary engineering plans that included the extension of Washington Avenue and city water and sewer lines into the Pine Bush. All of these were needed if the area was to be developed. Years after the development of the Pine Bush was underway Mayor Corning said, "The eventual development of the Pine Bush was guaranteed when the Thruway, Washington Avenue

Extension, Karner Road, sewer lines and water lines were built."[9]
In 1978 an *Albany Knickerbocker News* article titled "How to Make
$1 Million in the Pine Bush" discussed the probable development
of the Pine Bush area. "In retrospect, it seems almost inevitable
that the Pine Bush, Albany's last frontier, would attract this kind of
attention. For developers, the area certainly represented a source of
quicker profits than could be realized by rehabilitating a decaying
inner city."[10]

WASHINGTON AVENUE EXTENSION

The next major change that affected the Pine Bush and the Rapp
Road community was the building of the Washington Avenue
Extension, built in 1971. This four-lane road, which runs from
Karner Road in Colonie to Fuller Road where it joins the older
section of Washington Avenue, is approximately three miles long.
This road opened up the entire area to new development. Stores,
office buildings, condominiums, and nursing homes moved in. The
new road cut across the Rapp Road community separating the two
most northern homes, owned by Joshua Burney and William and
Gladys Robinson, from the rest of the community. William and
Libbie Toliver's house sat in the middle of where the Washington
Avenue Extension is today. State officials told them they had two
options: sell it, or move it. The Tolivers opted for the latter; the
state came and moved their house south about one hundred yards.
It now sits on the end of Rapp Road, house number 8.[11]

The new road through the community brought the first
development to the Pine Bush area. In a newspaper article, Rapp
Road resident Emma Dickson told the *Knickerbocker News*, "We
never had any traffic down this road. There were no strangers here
because the road was a dead end. It didn't go anywhere. Since they
built Washington Avenue and all those nursing homes, traffic down

this street has tripled."[12] Motorists use Rapp Road as a cut-across between Western Avenue and Washington Avenue Extension.

To help the community cope with noise pollution from Washington Avenue Extension, the state planted a single line of tall pine trees behind the houses that sit on the Frontage Road. (Frontage Road was created as an access road to Washington Avenue Extension.) Rapp Road residents claim that the single row of pine trees does not buffer out the noise from Washington Avenue Extension. If fact, residents say that on summer nights they can hear traffic from Washington Avenue Extension, the New York State Thruway, and I-87.[13]

With the new development came people who had no idea there was a black community living in the middle of the Pine Bush. Resident Emma Dickson remembers the public's reaction. "When Washington Avenue Extension went in, people would go by and look in awe and think they must be lost. I wonder what they [all these black families] are doing way out here in the woods? And they're just driving by looking at us all strange.... The same thing still happens today. People who don't know we're out here, or don't normally go out here.... If they see one person of color out on their lawn, they think OK, but as they go down the road, more than likely they are going to see more African Americans outside working on their lawn. Then they really start driving very slowly.... It surprises many people to see an African American community outside the city of Albany."[14] In addition to the commercial development from the Washington Avenue Extension there was the emergence of vandalism. Vandals hit the community several times ripping down resident's mailboxes, as well as street and traffic signs.[15] Also several times in the late 1970s and 1980s, carloads of teenagers drove through the community yelling racist slurs at community members.[16] Commenting on the situation in a newspaper article, Emma Dickson said, "change doesn't come easy in the Holy Land [Rapp Road community's residential nickname], neighborhood residents are quiet churchgoing people. They don't bother anybody and they don't want anybody to bother them."[17]

PYRAMID CROSSGATES CORPORATION

The greatest threat to the Rapp Road community came in the late 1970s with the Pyramid Crossgates Corporation shopping mall. The Pyramid Crossgates Company was a subsidiary of the Pyramid Corporation that was based in Syracuse, New York. The corporation had built several malls throughout Upstate New York, in Ithaca, Cortland, Syracuse, Utica, Glens Falls, and Saratoga County.[18] The company decided upon the Pine Bush area after seeing aerial photographs of the area. Clemmie Harris, a graduate student who investigated the environmental impact of the Crossgates mall wrote, "The aerial photographs identified an ideal location to Sproul [Robert Sproul, a former member of the Pyramid Crossgates Company development firm] on which to build the mall. He saw approximately 170 acres of undeveloped land just south of the New York State Thruway; north of Western Avenue (a main thoroughfare between the jurisdiction of Guilderland and Albany) and west of the Northway (I-87). This location made the Pine Bush accessible to highway travelers."[19] Furthermore, one of Crossgates' business partners, Bruce Kenan, already owned a hundred acres of land in the Pine Bush.[20]

In 1981 the *Knickerbocker News* published an article titled, "Blacks Fear Crossgates Mall Will Mean Change for 'Holy Land'." In the article, Emma Dickson served as the community spokesperson. She said, "The people out here [on Rapp Road] don't want trouble. They never put up a fuss because, so far, all the development's been over on Washington Avenue. But if they see something's going to come into the neighborhood and affect them, they're going to oppose it'."[21]

When the Pyramid Crossgates Corporation began surveying land in the late 1970s they took aerial photos of the Pine Bush and decided where they would build the giant mall and access roads. Between the time of the photographs and the development of the mall, Emma Dickson had built her house, located at 28 Rapp Road. Dickson's parents, Alfred and Leola Woodard, subdivided their plot of land for their daughter's home. Dickson recalled the incident with the corporation in an interview. "It was strange when they came because they said they were going to put a road through . . . and I said, 'I don't think so because you will be putting it on top of my driveway.' They told me that there was no house there. I said, 'I beg your pardon, there is, I live in it.' "[22] This was just the beginning of the fight between the Rapp Road community and the Pyramid Crossgates Corporation.

The developers sought to build the mall on a site bounded by Western Avenue, Washington Avenue Extension, Rapp Road, and the New York State Thruway. Shortly after the mall's proposal the community mobilized to save their land from the Crossgates developers. Rapp Road members began going to both Albany and Guilderland land zoning meetings in an effort to preserve their community. In an interview in April 2002 Emma Dickson remembered the stressful period. "We went to the hearings and we heard ourselves referred to as a small ethnic group, and that was the only mention. It is probable that the Pyramid Crossgates Corporation did not think the members on Rapp Road would be a threat. When they first decided to build out here they had no qualms about this community because they would just buy us up and we would disappear. Well they have been here quite some time now and we're still here, and they are still trying to make sure that we are gone."[23]

In the summer of 1981 the Guilderland Board of Zoning Appeals held three public hearings dealing with the building of the mall and its parking spaces. Rapp Road residents spoke at the second and third hearings. The second hearing took place on 29 July 1981 at Farnsworth Middle School in Guilderland drawing a crowd of 275.[24] A *Times Union* article the following morning described the crowd at the hearing as "ugly."[25] The newspaper also reported that at one point early in the evening Michael Shanley, one of Crossgates' lawyers, in an attempt to defuse the tension in the room, "jokingly pointed to the wall of the cafetorium of the Farnsworth Middle School, where a list of rules for student behavior in the lunchroom included the prohibition, 'Don't throw food or other objects.' No one laughed."[26]

Public sentiments at the hearings were about four to one against the building of the mall.[27] Supporters of the mall felt it would bring jobs and a solid tax base, while opponents believed the mall would result in increased traffic congestion, environmental damage, and would ruin Guilderland's quality of life.[28] Rapp Road resident Javan Owens, Sr., was the first from the community to speak out against the mall. The *Times Union* reported his testimony the following day. "The crowd; which had reacted vocally to many of the speakers, listened in silence as David [Javan] Owens, a member of a small black community on Rapp Road, told the board the mall will ruin everything his neighborhood stands for. 'Thirty-five years ago we looked for a quiet place to live,' he said. 'We found that place on Rapp Road. A few years ago they improved Rapp Road and my grandson was hit by a car. I don't have the money to move to another place. I'm opposed to the mall,' he said. 'If you can't stop it, tell me how I can get another place to live.' "[29] According to the Zoning Board of Appeals, Owens was also concerned about the increase in traffic, noise pollution, and air pollution.[30]

The third round of public hearings on the building of Crossgates also took place at the Farnsworth Middle School. At this session, Emma Dickson (then Emma Pinchback) spoke on behalf of the Rapp Road residents in opposition to the development.

According to the Zoning Board of Appeals minutes, Dickson was concerned about several things. "She stated she lived at the intersection of Rapp Road and Springsteen Road. Her one concern for herself and the other residents on Rapp Road was the traffic on and thru the road. At present there is more traffic than the road can handle or that should be going thru a rural road. Unless there is a solution from Crossgates this road will not be able to handle any more traffic. If there isn't a solution to the problem the residents are living on a suicidal road. If there is a solution, and we can be shown, then that is all the residents on Rapp Road are concerned about."[31]

Rapp Road residents were not the only people who felt that the Rapp Road community was threatened by the shopping mall. Francis Roberts, a longtime member of Guilderland's Zoning Board of Appeals, conducted public hearings on zoning changes requested by the Crossgates developers. Roberts felt sympathetic toward the Rapp Road community. In an interview with the *Knickerbocker News* Roberts said, "I'm interested in what their [Rapp Road community members] feelings are. I'm afraid there's going to be a hell of an impact on that community with the mall."[32] Frank Commisso, an Albany County legislator, discussed how he felt about the Crossgates mall development and the Rapp Road community. "As the mall itself was being developed I felt it [the Rapp Road community] was being encroached upon. In the later years, when the mall was up and going and they [Crossgates] looked to expand they did visit with many of the residents. Emma [Dickson], myself, and many of the residents went toe to toe with them, with a good end result. We had a lot of communication. We never made it an issue where we were charging after one another. We did it in a business-like fashion."[33]

The commercial development in the Pine Bush gave the community some leverage to acquire some city services. In 1979 Rapp Road residents petitioned the city of Albany to install sewer lines on their road.[34] By 1980 the city installed them. Also during this time the city installed water lines to the Rapp Road homes. Prior to this, residents used private wells and pumps to retrieve water. The water lines came just in time, because on 8 April 1981 at 10 a.m. a wildfire broke out in the Pine Bush and ten residents' homes on Pine Lane (the road that runs just off of Rapp Road on the Western Avenue side) burned down because there were no water hydrants for the firefighters to use.[35] Rapp Road residents dealt with the 1981 brush fire the same way they dealt with fires for years; they doused their homes with water in hopes that it would deter them from catching fire.[36]

According to his official mayoral documents pertaining to the development of the Pine Bush, Mayor Corning did not see the Rapp Road community members as an obstacle. In 1970 there were only fifty-two people living within Albany's city boundary in the Pine Bush. The majority of them were the Rapp Road community. The only mention in Corning's papers of the Rapp Road community came on 2 May 1979 when Daniel McCann was arrested and charged with operating an automobile repair garage and junkyard from his residentially zoned home.[37] Morton E. Jenkins, a partner of Wellspring Incorporated, wrote to Corning about the McCann property on Rapp Road: "The Wellspring House of Albany project (a residential counseling center for former members of religious cults) on Washington Avenue Extension is progressing on schedule. We expect to open for occupancy in late summer or early fall. One of our major problems is the cancer of the McCann property immediately adjacent on Rapp Road. Commissioner Plantz has been making a valiant effort to cure the problem. If your office could assist him in anyway, it would be greatly appreciated."[38] Eventually McCann complied with the zoning laws and cleaned up his property.

Rapp Road's location between two main corridors of the city, Western Avenue and Washington Avenue, made it an easy shortcut for the people who knew about it. Longtime resident Labor Johnson felt that by 1987 "There's already too much traffic for a residential neighborhood."[39] To make matters worse, in the summer of 1987 the town of Guilderland proposed moving the entrance of Rapp Road west about 300 feet so it would meet with Johnston Road and then adding a half-mile of road east off Rapp Road so it would connect with Crossgates Mall Road.[40] This plan suggested that traffic on Western Avenue would be substantially reduced because westbound traffic would use Rapp Road and Crossgates Mall Road to get to Washington Avenue Extension and the Northway (I-87). Also, traffic traveling southbound on the Northway would get off at Crossgates Mall and cut through to Rapp Road instead of getting off at Western Avenue.[41] Rapp Road residents were opposed to the plan. First-generation resident Hosea Fairley was quoted in a newspaper article as saying, "'I don't like it at all simply because it will mean more traffic. . . . As it is now, my 5-year-old daughter can't cross the road.'" But the article went on to say that he "said that even if he and his 12 neighbors fought the change, it wouldn't make a difference. 'We didn't want Crossgates here,' Fairley said, pointing across the street to the mall, hidden behind a wall of trees. 'We protested something awful and it did very little good.'"[42] Eventually the town of Guilderland decided to scrap its plans because commercial developers had other plans for the area.

In 1994 the Pyramid Crossgates Corporation and Conseco Mortgage Capital Incorporated added a large shopping plaza, known as a power center, northwest of the Crossgates mall called Crossgates Commons. The complex contained the first superstores to open in the Capitol Region, such as a large Wal-Mart, Sam's Club, Home Depot, Old Navy, MJ Designs, and Media Play.[43] (A superstore is a store almost twice the size of a regular store that carries a large assortment of routinely purchased items.) Originally, Crossgates Commons was to be 420,000 square feet, but in March

1994 the owners decided to expand the complex to 640,000 by adding another building.

The Crossgates Commons complex is about one-tenth of a mile north of the Rapp Road community; it sits just on the other side of Washington Avenue Extension. Emma Dickson recalled in an interview how the building of Crossgates Commons affected her community. "There were homes on the other side where Crossgates Commons is, and if you look there today, you would never know there was a residential community there. There are three pieces of the original lots, of the twenty-two lots that were originally bought, that were divided from Rapp Road when the Washington Avenue Extension went through. Those three pieces ended up being on the other side of Washington Avenue Extension and are now commercial property and the houses demolished."[44] The Rapp Road homes that Dickson referred to were Joshua Burney's and William and Gladys Robinson's, which were separated from the community by Washington Avenue Extension. The third property Dickson referred to was that of William and Libbie Toliver, who had their house moved forward because it sat in the way of Washington Avenue Extension. Today the west side of Home Depot's parking lot is the site where the two houses and part of the Toliver's property sat.[45]

As a result of the new development around the Pine Bush in 1993 the Niagara Mohawk Power Corporation proposed to put a 13.2 kilovolt substation on a vacant land parcel on the west side of the street between Gipp Road and Pine Lane.[46] This plot of land was very close to the homes on Rapp Road. Residents on and around Rapp Road were upset for both health and financial reasons; owners felt the market value of their land would drop with a giant power station so near. The utility claimed it needed to upgrade its power grid to accommodate all of the new commercial development in the area.[47] Residents were so upset and raised such a fuss that Niagara Mohawk postponed the project for a year and then decided it was better to change locations than fight the community.[48] Local newspapers referred to the ordeal as a David and Goliath story.

Pyramid Crossgates Corporation development in the Pine Bush area continued for several more years, much to the Rapp Road community's concern. In April 1993, the mall began an expansion project that increased its size to roughly 1.5 million square feet.[49] This expansion included the straightening of the southern section of Rapp Road and making it into part of the Crossgates ring road extension.[50] After this expansion an opinion letter in the *Times Union* appeared titled, "Rapp Road Never Meant to Be a Real Through Road."[51] Steven Sweeney wrote, "At that time [when part of Rapp Road became Crossgates Mall Road] the local community became concerned over the potential volume of traffic that could take advantage of the local road system. It was feared that the small-community feel of Rapp and Gipp roads would be lost in the rush of 'just passing through' cars, and at the same time make the area less safe for vehicles, pedestrians, and children. Rapp Road is designed strictly as a local-usage road, not as a through road."[52]

In the late 1990s the corporation began buying parcels of land around the Crossgates mall.[53] The hope of this large corporation was to expand the Crossgates mall from 1.6 million square feet to 3.6 million square feet with parking decks, a hotel, amusement facilities, three additional wings, and hundreds more stores.[54] Again the public was split. Supporters felt the expansion would help Albany's tax base revenue and place the region on the map as having one of the largest shopping malls in the nation.[55] The people against the expansion felt that it would force smaller stores and hotels in the area to close down, create traffic problems, noise pollution, and air pollution. Barbara Quint of Guilderland wrote in an opinion piece for the *Times Union*, "No, we're not imagining it. No, we're not being hysterical. We don't want the Crossgates expansion in Guilderland and we're not crazy. This proposal, should it come to pass, would dominate our whole town. The sheer size of this mammoth structure and its surrounding would be the town and our private dwellings would be like the rings around Saturn, circling the planet. It would not be Guilderland anymore, but the town of Crossgates with some dwellings nearby."[56]

During this time Pyramid Crossgates Corporation bought pieces of the Rapp Road community, no matter what the size. They even purchased small tracts of land between houses. Ultimately, they wanted to connect all their land purchases together. In an interview, community spokesperson Emma Dickson recalled this traumatic time in the community's history. "Right now we are the only residential piece that stands between them [Pyramid Crossgates Corporation] and the commercial office buildings on Washington Avenue Extension. They own Western Avenue all the way back to Gipp Road. They have a good portion of Washington Avenue. We are the thing in their way that is residential. They are now trying to rezone pieces of Rapp Road to commercial. We are trying really hard to make sure that does not happen. . . . So we are working very hard right now to make sure Crossgates does not get any of the residential pieces on this side of Rapp Road."[57]

During this time, if there was a vacant house or a first-generation resident passed away, the community would get nervous about losing another property to the corporation. Community members took matters into their own hands. If a house became vacant or had the possibility of becoming vacant soon, phone calls were made to find someone to move in or to continue paying taxes on the property so it would not go up for sale. Residents also were offered large amounts of money to sell their property to developers, but the answer was always no. In an interview Frank Commisso, Albany County Legislator, discussed meeting with community members about selling their property.

> These are children of their ancestors who lived out there and farmed the land, and had animals and so on and so forth. My

impression is that these kids that now took title to these properties and the old folks that are still there have taken such an interest in the area that it is coming from the heart. It's not dollar value. I mean they could get mega dollars for some of that land. I went over that with them at one point. I said, you know what you're saying [about selling their property to developers]? They said, "NO! We are not interested." I said fine, I just want you to know all the possibilities here. I sat down with them all at a meeting at Emma's [Dickson] home.[58]

When asked in a newspaper article why he should do whatever he could to protect the Rapp Road community, first-generation Rapp Road resident Alfred Woodard said, "'This [Rapp Road] has been very good to me.'"[59] As of 2004, the Pyramid Crossgates Company owned five lots in the Rapp Road community; they are 7 Rapp Road, 13 Rapp Road, 62 Rapp Road, 66 Rapp Road, and 70 Rapp Road.

County Legislator Commisso had a plan for the community if the mall expanded. He proposed changing Rapp Road at Pine Lane to a one-way road going back to Western Avenue.[60] This would route commuters away from the community and they would have to drive all the way around to get to either Washington Avenue or Western Avenue. Commisso felt that the community, at that point, had put up with developers long enough.[61]

Ultimately the expansion of the Crossgates mall never materialized because in 1999 Guilderland zoning laws squashed the project; town laws limited malls to one million square feet.[62] Furthermore, plans were widely protested by both Albany and Guilderland residents who feared the larger mall would create many problems. Yet Rapp Road members did not breathe a sigh of relief when the Crossgates mall cancelled its expansion plans and even began selling off its Pine Bush property in 2001.[63] Many residents still felt that another commercial developer could come along with plans to buy out the black community.

As a result of the commercial development all around the Rapp Road community, the residents have acquired a type of siege mentality toward outsiders snooping around their area. On several occasions land developers and surveyors appeared on residents' land and took photographs and measurements without permission from the landowners. A neighborhood watch was established and if any stranger showed up in the community for any reason they were soon questioned and asked to leave.

By 2000, development around the Rapp Road community seemed to be at a standstill. Although Washington Avenue Extension and Crossgates Commons were visible from the community, tall pine trees and other vegetation blocked sight of the Crossgates mall. This was only true in daylight hours, because at night Crossgates' parking lot lights lighted up the Rapp Road community. Despite all this, the community was still intact and thriving. Second- and third-generation members moved back to Rapp Road and refurbished the homes they grew up in. Community members were aware of what they had almost lost and began seriously thinking about how to stop another land grab. Community member Emma Dickson felt that a historic district designation could help preserve her community for the future.

CHAPTER 5

"I Needed to Let People Know the Community Was Here"

From a historic standpoint [the Rapp Road community] is kind of funny. I remember the first time I ever actually drove through it. I got out of the car and walked it. It was the first time I was convinced that this really was an important place. Which is kind of funny because I read your text [the research paper the book developed from] and I read other accounts and still had a lot of trepidation that this was something I could not sell [to the New York State Board for Historic Preservation]. When I actually walked it, there is a feeling back there—it's palpable. When you get out of the car and begin walking the roads, you really get a sense that this place is very foreign from the rest of the city of Albany, Colonie, and the region. There is a sense in the set back, in the way the houses are designed, in their scale, in their orientation—it's a different place. I think that becomes the real character-defining feature for that community. From a historic standpoint that is the most important thing about Rapp Road.

—John Bonafide, New York State Historic Preservation Services Coordinator, in a 24 February 2004 interview with the author

The Rapp Road community withstood the Pine Bush land grab, the development of Washington Avenue Extension, the Crossgates mall, and Crossgates Commons. Residents knew that they were vulnerable targets for future developers and commercialization. To help her neighborhood, community leader Emma Dickson turned to public history to help document, preserve, and ultimately save the Rapp Road community from outside forces.

Historically, the application of African American history arose out of the desire to promote a positive racial identity among blacks, to challenge racist stereotypes, and to preserve a history in danger of being lost.[1] African American history served the needs of the black community by acting as its cultural defender and debating the merits of integration and separation. Furthermore, this type of history tended to prosper during times of social change when African Americans found history as a means of coping with social upheaval. In the case of the Rapp Road community, the application of public history practices in the form of a historic district designation served as a vehicle to promote, preserve, and protect this African American community.

In 1997 the New York State Office of Parks, Recreation, and Historic Preservation published the *Guide to the Survey of Historical Resources Associated with African Americans in New York State* because African American historic sites were underrepresented in the state. African American historic preservation was overlooked in New York State for several reasons. The contemporary historic preservation movement, which grew out of the establishment of the National Historic Landmarks program in the early 1930s, recognized and protected history and monuments that were defined by the majority cultural group, in this case European Americans.[2] Much of the preservation activity of state and local history revolved around properties significant for their visual and architectural qualities. Unfortunately, architectural resources were often evaluated solely in terms of their design quality and measured against the standards of European American architectural history.[3] Historians who relied on broad, general contexts overlooked historic properties whose significance was revealed in terms of local history, and some preservationists were uncomfortable with protecting resources that represented the cruelty or repression of a specific group in history. It is fortunate that the Rapp Road community sought a historical designation during a new era in New York State historic preservation.

The New York State Historic Preservation Office defines three phases that researchers should follow when identifying and evaluating property types related to African American history. Phase I consists of archival research and analysis: "The product of this phase is a preliminary overview based on archival research that summarizes the history of the area, analyzes the results of previous survey work and reaches conclusions about its quality, and seeks to make general predictions about which portions of the survey area are likely to contain different types of historic resources."[4] Phase II consists of the field study where a surveyor verifies the initial historical research of Phase I and looks for additional information. The final phase, Phase III, is a review and organization of the survey data. It is in this stage that all the collected data is assembled into a report and evaluated to identify whether the property meets the State and National Register criteria.[5] Phase III specifically addresses concerns stemming from evaluating an African American property differently than a European American property.

> African-Americans were placed in special strata in American society, in American politics, and in the American capitalist structure. Because of this, if we assign greater or lesser worth to a resource based on its recognition by the larger contemporary society, we will be collaborating in turning African Americans into an invisible people. If we want to change this, we must first recognize the fact that for three hundred years African Americans were acting out their lives and coping in ways germane to their survival. Therefore, those deciding on the value of historic resources may have to respond to the more restrictive question, "were these sites significant in the lives of these people?"[6]

This attempt to place African Americans into the criteria for the State and National Register is fitting for African American properties and especially appropriate for a community like Rapp

Road because without these new criteria, the Rapp Road area would have been ignored.

In 1998, New York State boasted more than 4,000 properties listed on the State and National Register of Historic Places. Of this vast quantity, only 48 were associated with African American history.[7] The majority of these properties are located in New York County and were homes of famous African Americans such as Langston Hughes, Duke Ellington, James Weldon Johnson, Charlie Parker, and Paul Robeson.[8] Outside of New York County, the bulk of historic properties associated with African Americans deal with black churches and African American cemeteries. Only one of the historic properties in New York, the Durham Memorial A.M.E. Zion Church in Buffalo, dealt with the Great Migration.

On a national level the dedication to African American historic sites is similar to that of New York State. Currently, the National Register of Historic Places boasts more than 77,000 properties, with only about 1,200 properties based on their significance to African American history.[9] The National Register of Historic Places, which is maintained by the National Park Service, is our nation's inventory of historic districts, sites, buildings, structures, and objects significant in American history, architecture, archeology, engineering, and culture.[10] The National Register includes nationally significant historic areas of the National Parks System, important National Historic Landmarks, and state and federal agency nominations. Of the state and federal agency nominations, more than 90 percent of them are of state and local significance.[11] The majority of the African American historic sites on the National Register deal with architecture, black churches, black-owned businesses, education, the plantation system, slavery, and black colleges.

Historic properties relating to the Great Migration are scant. By the mid-1990s there were only seven registered historic places that specifically dealt with the history of the Great Migration.[12] Among the seven properties is Robert S. Abbot House in Chicago,

Illinois, which was noted because the namesake of the home was the creator of the *Chicago Defender*, a black newspaper that encouraged thousands of African Americans to migrate north during the early twentieth century. The Bethany Baptist Church in Newark, New Jersey, which provided services to the ever-increasing black population during the Great Migration, is a registered property.[13] The Durham Memorial A.M.E. Zion Church in Buffalo, New York, served as the focal point of educational, social, political, and religious activities for the southern migrants upon entry in Buffalo.[14] The Langston Terrace Dwellings, located in Washington, D.C., was built by the Works Progress Administration between 1935 and 1938 and marks the beginning of federally sponsored low-income housing in the United States. This particular complex was created as a result of the large influx of poor black migrants to the D.C. area in the first few decades of the twentieth century.[15] The Liberty Baptist Church located in Evansville, Indiana, served migrants' needs throughout the mid-nineteenth and twentieth centuries. The Wabash Avenue YMCA, in Chicago, Illinois, staff members assisted new migrants from the South in finding housing, employment, and temporary rooms.[16] Lastly, the St. Mark's African Methodist Church in Duluth, Minnesota, is listed as a historic site dealing with the Great Migration, but does not seem to fit into that category. This historic church is the only public building in the city built by and for African Americans. This church hosted W. E. B. Du Bois in 1921 to encourage the establishment of a NAACP chapter in Duluth.[17] The Rapp Road community, although a product of the Great Migration, is different from these historic places because it is an entire community that is still intact and thriving with original migrants and their descendants.

In the early 1970s, when Washington Avenue extension was built, second-generation Rapp Road resident Emma Dickson felt that her community was in danger of being lost to development. Dickson's first efforts to help preserve the community were through education. "I needed to let people know that the community was here, because if they didn't know that it existed then there would be no chance in saving it. I had to make sure I started educating people about it and communicating about it, in order to just let them know it existed because most of Albany, and that's African Americans and whites, had no idea about it or that this community existed.[18] Dickson attended both Guilderland town meetings and Albany Common Council meetings because, although the community is in the city of Albany, Guilderland bounds it. At these meetings Dickson spoke about the community and why she thought it was important: "In my opinion I did not feel that there was another community in the Capital District area like Rapp Road, or had been settled like Rapp Road had. It was important that people knew exactly how it was settled and knew the truth about why they came here and settled it. . . . Although some people had heard rumors about it, I don't think there were any facts about the settlement."[19]

In addition to speaking at public meetings, Dickson began talking to the older members on Rapp Road to get their personal stories of why they moved to Albany and what life was like in Shubuta. In the mid-1970s, it was important for Dickson to talk to the original settlers on Rapp Road because she knew they would not be around much longer.[20] At that point, most of the residents on Rapp Road appreciated Dickson taking an interest in their history, but did not feel that their homes were threatened in any way by development.

It was not until the late 1970s when the Pyramid Crossgates Corporation held planning meetings about the building of the mall that the settlers on Rapp Road thought their community could actually disappear.[21] Dickson and fellow community members attended planning meetings. Dickson remembered, "Every time they [Crossgates developers] came up with a new plan, which they did. Today you might be looking at Plan A, but the developers had changed it and were already on Plan B and Plan C. So what I had to do was keep up with their plans and make sure they were not going to do anything that said roads, egress roads. Or make sure none of their buildings were going to come into this community. . . . Had we not been going to the meetings—at one point there was an egress road that went right into our community—had we not been going to the meetings, we never would have known about the road."[22] At this point Dickson recruited neighbors from outside the community on Pine Lane and Gipp Road. She told the Pine Lane and Gipp Road residents, "What happens to us, happens to you. So you need to start going to these meetings."[23]

Dickson continued attending planning meetings to find out the corporation's building plans and to share her community's history. In 1995, Dickson turned to history to see if something could be done to help the community:

> I looked at the city [of Albany]. The first thing I thought of historically was contacting the city. I knew about the city's historic buildings, but when I looked at when the city did their historic preservation, it just seemed to me that they were single buildings and there were very strict guidelines, like not being able to change the color of the house, just very strict guidelines. I knew the residents of this community were not going to go for that, so I started looking for the next step. If I couldn't get it through the city, then I would try to get something through the state. I started calling around. I had no idea who to contact at the state. I knew it was there, but did not know who to contact. So I called New York State Historic Preservation; they asked me where was I located. I told them what I was looking for . . . I was put in contact with Kathleen LaFrank.[24]

State Historic Preservation Office (SHPO) staff members Kathleen LaFrank and Vic DiSanto visited Dickson at her home on 28 Rapp Road. Dickson told the SHPO staff members the history of the Rapp Road settlement. Dickson remembered that first meeting in an interview. "I sat down and told her [LaFrank] the story. She had no idea of the story, none whatsoever. She then said to me, 'We have been actively looking for African American sites, you have come along at a good time because there has been a new criteria written up for those sites, a new cultural criteria, and from what you told me, some of that might fit into that new criteria.' So we walked the road in the pouring rain and she was a good sport about it and I told her the story [of the community]."[25] At the end of the tour LaFrank advised Dickson to document the community's history. LaFrank also told Dickson she felt the community was worthy of a New York State historic designation. Dickson recalled this in an interview: "She [LaFrank] said to me, 'you might have a good chance of having this become a historic district, for one thing on the mere fact that you are still here.' She said, 'We have gone out, people have called us to come and look at African American sites, or what had been African American sites and we [SHPO staff members] get there and there is nothing there.' So she said, 'the big difference with yours is that you're still here and it's thriving.' "[26]

After the initial meeting about a Rapp Road historic designation, Dickson sought out Albany public historians, Wesley Balla, the history curator at the Albany Institute of History & Art, and Stefan Bielinski, community historian at the New York State Museum. Both Balla's and Bielinski's responses about the community were positive. Eventually, Balla went out to Rapp Road to take photographs and take Dickson's history tour of the community. Balla was the first historian to begin public records research on the community. Bielinski encouraged Dickson to get her story out in the public. Dickson began giving public presentations on the history of the community and her experiences growing up in it. Dickson recalled some audience responses from her public presentations. "When I spoke at Hackett Middle School the audience was mixed, black and white. Except for when I spoke at churches—black churches—the audiences were mostly white. Their reactions were very surprised. They were surprised that the community existed. They had no idea we were out there."[27]

By 2000, Dickson wanted to get the nomination process moving. She realized she needed help writing the historical nomination for the community, but did not know who would write it. Although Bielinski and Balla were obvious choices to write the nomination, their busy work schedules prevented them from focusing on the Rapp Road community. In an interview Dickson recalls this time. "I started thinking, who am I going to contact to help me with this? As I was looking at this list [of possible historians] I got a call from Wayne Jackson. Wayne Jackson is my cousin that my father raised; he grew up with us on 22 Rapp Road. He is now the Sergeant at Arms in the New York State Assembly. Wayne called and said, 'there is a young woman here who Jack [John J.] McEneny [New York State Assemblyman] sent to talk to me, but I am sending her to talk to you.' And that is when Jennifer [Lemak] enters the picture."[28] Then a graduate student at the University of Albany, I was interested in writing a research paper on the community. After speaking with Dickson about a historic designation, I felt that such a research paper could serve as the basis for the nomination process.

The development in and around the Rapp Road area gave the residents a siege mentality toward outsiders. Often visitors to the community would be immediately asked what their business was on Rapp Road, and if it had anything to do with land speculation or real estate they were usually asked to leave. Dickson was a little apprehensive of me when I first phoned. She recalled, "I wanted to know what exactly she was doing, why she was doing it, how she was going to do it, and if she was earnest about doing it. I knew how the people in this community are and whether or not they would let her interview them. That was a concern of mine. I thought this because she was not from this community.

Because of the Crossgates thing, they [Rapp Road residents] were very suspicious, suspicious of everything and everyone. Unless you were a part of this community or they knew you very well for years and years, they did not trust you."[29]

Dickson and I went right to work collecting the community's history. There was little information about African American life in Albany, and except for a few newspaper articles, nothing documented the Rapp Road community. I explained that I would have to conduct oral history interviews with community members and church members. Dickson recalled how she approached the community about me conducting interviews.

> I knew it was not going to work if Jennifer just called them [community members] up and said, 'I'm Jennifer Lemak, gradu-ate student.' So what I did was I called them up, people that I thought she should go and interview and I would explain what we were doing and why we were doing it. I explained her part of it and I explained how it was going to benefit us in this com-munity. I asked them if they would agree to have her come and interview them. I told them that I would not be coming with her. It worked. . . . I was honest with them [community members] and told them she is writing a paper, but we need this informa-tion, and we need this documented because they knew what I wanted to do. I think once they started telling her the stories they really got into it.[30]

After several oral history interviews, I wrote my research paper on the history of the Rapp Road community; this paper eventually served as the basis for the historical nomination.

In the summer of 2000 Dickson began working with John Bonafide, a New York State Historic Preservation Services Coordinator, to determine whether the Rapp Road community could be worthy of a historic register designation. In an interview Bonafide recalled that his first impressions of the community was, "not good. I had driven past it on a bunch of occasions and looking at it not from a historian's standpoint, but from a process standpoint—how would you get something like this listed?" He continued,

> The initial reaction was that it was just not going to work; our board would not be sympathetic to this type of property. They [the board] tend to be very visually oriented. There is no clean exciting visual that one can take away from Rapp that would have met their standard. Any work that was put into it would have resulted in the board saying "no," so from a process standpoint it was a negative. From a historian's standpoint it really did intrigue me, the story that came out of it really excited me and I wished we had a board that was a little more open minded that we could craft a case to get through the system on.[31]

Dickson and Bonafide had several more challenges to face besides the New York State Historic Registry Board of Directors.

The first major hurdle that faced this project was the documentation of the history of the community. The nomination had to identify which criteria were significant to the property. In the case of the Rapp Road Historic District, criteria A and B were relevant to its historic evaluation. Criterion A includes properties that are associated with events that have made a significant contribution to the broad patterns of our history.[32] The Rapp Road community is included in this criterion because it is an end product of the Great Migration. Criterion B includes properties that are associated with the lives of persons significant in our past, in this case, the community's association with Reverend Louis W. Parson.[33] Next, Bonafide suggested a different approach to document the houses in the community. Bonafide recalled, "the individuals' histories, which is one of the things we decided to use when we talked about each of the buildings because architecturally the buildings had very little to offer. So when we designed the architectural piece of this, the building list, we actually created a personal narrative of each building that was based on the history of the people who built it.

It was a very unique approach."[34] Eventually, all of the written materials were collected and assembled for the New York State Historic Preservation Board.

The next obstacle Dickson faced was to make sure Rapp Road property owners were willing to allow their property to be included in the proposed historic district. Dickson remembered, "I knew this was not going to be an easy sell because, even with me, the one thing they [Rapp Road residents] are very suspicious of is their land. Because they had to sacrifice so hard to obtain this land, they will hold on to it at all costs. If they thought anything was going to jeopardize that land, they were not going to agree to it."[35] To help educate the Rapp Road residents about the historic registry and the nomination process, Dickson asked Bonafide to come speak to the residents and answer their questions. In the winter of 2001 Rapp Road residents went to a meeting at Dickson's house to discuss the nomination process. Dickson recalled the meeting. "John [Bonafide] and Jennifer [Lemak] were here and I think every resident on the road was here. John explained to them exactly what it meant, that it did not mean that they would not be able to sell their land if they wanted to do that. It did not mean, as it would with the city historic properties, that they could not change their properties. He dispelled a lot of the myths. Because a lot of these homes were so old they needed repair work done on them [residents] felt that if that [repair of their property] was something they could not do they would have said no to the nomination."[36]

Bonafide also felt that community support was imperative. "The harder part of Rapp Road [nomination]" he recalled, "was defining a clear boundary for it, getting neighborhood support for it, and convincing the people who live there, other than Emma Dickson, that it was something they should consider doing and putting it on the National Register was not going to have a negative impact on them."[37] Bonafide felt the Rapp Road residents had initial fears similar to that of other historic registry property owners. The biggest fear was that a big government was going to come in and take over their property.[38] The big question asked at the meeting was, "What is the nomination going to do for me?" Bonafide's response was frank.

> The reality is nothing. I don't think it [a historic designation] would increase the property value on Rapp Road, which it tends to do in a lot of other communities because I think the property value on Rapp Road is simply the value that Pyramid Corporation places on it acquiring each of those lots. They [Rapp Road residents] are always going to get more through a corporate sale than they would if they were to sell to another homeowner. In this case there were really no financial incentives; it was really a matter of pride. That was the direction we worked with, with Emma and her neighbors. This is a way of recognizing what their parents and grandparents had done, and it was really that simple. I think that is really the approach that Emma had sought from the beginning. It worked well.[39]

At the conclusion of the meeting, every Rapp Road resident was on board with the nomination.

Bonafide had to finesse this nomination into fruition. Pyramid Crossgates Corporation, owning property on and around Rapp Road, most likely could have stopped the nomination from passing, or at the very least held it up indefinitely. The Crossgates property was a concern for Bonafide. "We were faced with the political realization that we had a major potential problem with an adjoining landowner, who, if they chose to object the listing would really cause irrevocable damage for this to move forward. So part of the process became a political negotiation with the Pyramid Development Corporation who were very good about it. Luckily, Emma Dickson had wrestled with them before, and won, and they knew her and I think were slightly afraid of dealing with her. It became a negotiation on our part too."[40] It is possible that the Pyramid Crossgates Corporation had concerns about the nomination also. Bonafide recalled his past dealings with large development companies. "When we are talking about National Register and developers, generally, what we find is that they have a lot of fear because if a corporation like that is dealing with a large land acquisition and development there is always permitting involved and state and federal permits. Having to acquire a piece of land that is on the National Register triggers a much higher level of environmental review and also has to go through the state and local laws . . . so it can slow them down, its not going to stop development, but it can redesign development."[41]

Bonafide had to make decisions about properties to exclude from the historic district. He remembered, "This resulted in a gap-tooth boundary. Normally we would not have taken sections of most districts out, but in this case it was the most expeditious way to deal with it [Pyramid Crossgates land] rather than have Pyramid object or possibly object."[42] In addition to the Pyramid Crossgates Corporation's land the properties at 53 Rapp Road and 21 Rapp Road were removed from the district because their character was greatly altered. A condominium development is located at 53 Rapp Road, and 21 Rapp Road is the site of an Association of Retarded Citizens home.

One of the last tasks of the nomination process was to collect letters of support for the proposed historic district. Bonafide felt this was an important aspect of the Rapp Road nomination. Dickson, Bonafide, and I gathered seventeen letters of support from local and state political leaders, public historians, academics, leaders of race organizations, and community members. Most New York State nominations only have two to three letters of support.

After Dickson and I assembled our nomination materials and handed them into the State Office of Historic Preservation, Bonafide prepared the nomination's paperwork and continued to educate the Historic Preservation Board of Trustees. The nomination was scheduled to go up for review in 2001, but Bonafide decided to put it off. He recalled, "It took a long time. The initial problem was that I don't think there was a lot of strong belief that if we tried to propel it forward it would go. So we really tried not to get people's hopes up until we were convinced that we could make a case. . . . As we got closer to presenting it to the board, some of that delay was my own fear. I wanted to make sure we had strong letters of support. That we had all the owners on board, that we had politicians on board, that we had historians on board, and that we had good strong letters to bring to the Commissioner."[43] Bonafide also wanted to wait until the New York State Board for Historic Preservation quarterly meeting was convening near Albany so the Rapp Road residents could attend.

Finally, on Friday, 13 September 2002 at the Oakwood Cemetery in Troy, New York, the Rapp Road community's historic register nomination was scheduled for a board vote. The meeting took place at the Oakwood Cemetery crematorium because it, too, was on the list of historic register nominations that day. Dickson remembers the day vividly.

> The day we went there I was a little nervous because, first of all, it was in the cemetery, as we went in and sat down there were several nominations before ours. I kept thinking, "Oh, just hurry up, just hurry up!" As we sat there they started going through all these building nominations. I started realizing, just as John Bonafide had told us, that it was an unusual nomination. Jennifer [Lemak] and I kept asking him [Bonafide], "when is this going to nomination? When is this going to nomination?" He [Bonafide] just kept telling us to take it slow so when it does go to nomination they [the historic preservation board] understand this type of nomination that is coming before them. It was important to him [Bonafide] that they [the board] understand the type of nomination that was coming before them because it was the first time this type of nomination came before the board. So as I sat there I'm looking at all these different building nominations and

some of these buildings were just beautiful, and I'm thinking, "Oh my God they are going to look at our nomination and they are not going to understand what it was that we were trying to present them." As they moved along with the nominations ours finally came up. John Bonafide used family pictures in his presentation . . . as he presented the slides, he talked about the history of the community and why he though it was significant. The vote that day was unanimous.[44]

Dickson was elated that the nomination passed, but she was not the only one. "One of our original settlers was there that day," she related, "Mr. Fantroy, he is in his eighties, after the nomination was passed, he sat there with tears in his eyes and said that he felt that he 'would never live long enough to see this day come.' "[45] The nomination was important to Bonafide as well. He remembered how different this nomination was:

From a process standpoint I think it was one of the most unique nominations I got to work with because of the fact that I had to package it differently. It wasn't just talking about architecture when you describe fifteen or twenty buildings and each building has a style that you can talk about. It became talking about the people, and each building really is a representation of the families who put them there. That was a real unique approach taken on this nomination from a technical standpoint. I also think that getting the support from Pyramid [Crossgates Corporation] and getting very strong community support and very strong legislative support for the district I think were all really good. I also think crafting a presentation for the board [of trustees] was something I really enjoyed doing. Instead of focusing on images of architecture, I focused on images of people and really tried to hammer home the idea that this is not about pretty, it's not about what is aesthetically pleasing, it's about what is culturally important here. I think the board really saw it and bought into it and were really supportive of it.[46]

New York State Historic Preservation Board member John Scherer agreed that the Rapp Road nomination was different from other nominations that the board approves. Scherer said, "It was a good nomination and very different from typical nominations, which are buildings, church buildings, or homes that show great styles of architecture. We do historic districts, but they are usually very urban orientated. New York City has several historic districts that have been put on the register. Quaint villages are also put on the register, so yes the Rapp Road nomination was very different, but very appropriate. I was happy to see this sort of thing go on the register because something like this is not always recognized."[47] Scherer felt that the Board of Historic Preservation liked the Rapp Road Community's nomination because it was so unusual.[48] He also felt that the board would like to see more nominations of this nature. Scherer said, "This is the type of thing we would like to see more of, more of a grassroots type of thing rather than the high end examples we put on the register. I also think it was meaningful for the people who live there, to have it recognized as something special."[49]

The Rapp Road Historic District was the first historic register nomination in New York State that dealt with the Great Migration. In an interview, Bonafide summed up why this nomination was a first for New York State. "It is the first nomination of its type. It is the first nomination that deals with transplanted African Americans creating an enclave that replicates something approximating what they left in Mississippi. There are other sites in the state that have cultural importance as individual places, but I don't believe there is a grouping of buildings or community that represent that very important period in American history and I really think that although it was listed at state significance, I think that ultimately it can be justified at national significance when more research is done."[50]

In January 2003, four months after the Rapp Road Historic District was added to the New York State Historic Register, it was added to the National Register of Historic Places. This national designation was awarded in the context of statewide significance.

Once a nomination is added to the National Register of Historic Places it is categorized in a local, state, or national context. In order for the Rapp Road Historic District to be designated as significant in a national context, research had to be done on Great Migration settlements across the country to define how the Rapp Road community fits in.

There are many benefits the historic district designations offer the Rapp Road community. John Bonafide summarized the most important one in an interview. "I think the sense of pride that these people can now say, 'We were right!' This area is a place that is very, very important to the people of this state and we were not just kidding when we were telling you that as we were fighting off the people trying to overrun this property."[51] In addition to a sense of pride, the historic designations offer the community a level of protection against further expansion. It does not guarantee that government or private developers can never impact the community; it simply brings a higher level of environmental review. If a developer needs a state or federal permit to build his/her project, the SHPO office will help determine the issuance of the building permit.[52] In an interview, Emma Dickson discussed what she believed to be the biggest benefit of the historic designations. "For me personally, it means that what I have been saying all along has now been documented. It's there. No one years from now can say, 'Maybe it was there.' . . . It means that my parents and the people that settled here had the courage and made the sacrifices to do what they did, the nominations are a thing of respect for them."[53] Furthermore, the historic designations have instilled a sense of pride for the entire community. Community members now refer to Rapp Road as the Rapp Road Historic District.[54]

The New York State Rapp Road Historic District will retain this designation until the character-defining features that put it on the register disappear. In this case it is the setting, the orientation of the buildings, and the buildings themselves that helped put this community on the register. If the homes are torn down and the road is all that is left of the community, the SHPO office will reevaluate the district and most likely remove it from the historic register.[55]

MORE APPLICATIONS OF PUBLIC HISTORY
FOR THE RAPP ROAD COMMUNITY

After the historic district designations were official, the Capital Region slowly began to take notice of the Rapp Road community. Months after the historic designations, newspaper articles appeared in the *Albany Times Union*, the *Daily Gazette* (Schenectady), and the *Metroland* (Albany) newspapers. The major theme that emerged from these articles was the idea of this little-known community fighting to protect its history, winning the battle, and as a reward, receiving the historic district designations. Dickson continued lecturing on the history of the community and her experiences growing up there. The number of organizations wanting to hear Dickson increased, especially during February, Black History Month. The New York State Museum, the Albany Public Library, the Albany County Historical Association, and the Albany Institute of History & Art were all venues of Dickson's Rapp Road lecture.

In March 2003 the Albany County Historical Association's (ACHA) executive director, Brian Buff, asked Dickson if the Rapp Road community could be included in their seasonal exhibit, The Tapestry of Albany County: A Sampler of Historic Communities. Dickson agreed and asked community members if they had any objects to loan for the exhibit. Only a couple residents responded, so Dickson gathered objects from her family members for the exhibit. Several residents felt that they did not own anything of importance for a museum exhibit. The exhibit opened with a colorful panel of community and family photographs along with a history of the community. In front of the panel was a small case of objects from Rapp Road. Dickson and a few other community members attended the exhibit opening and were proud that Rapp Road was represented. Word of mouth around Rapp Road spread about the exhibit and the following day Dickson received several calls from community members with objects for the exhibit. Dickson contacted Buff about the new objects for the already opened exhibit. A few days later Buff reorganized the entire exhibit to add the new Rapp Road objects.

In fall 2003 I began working with the New York State Museum to create an exhibit about the Rapp Road community. This time when Dickson was contacted to see if community members had objects for an exhibit, the residents were much more receptive to loaning objects for a display. In October 2003, the New York State Museum opened the exhibit Bound for the Promised Land: The History of Albany's Rapp Road Community. Dickson and I opened the exhibit with a public presentation and gallery tour.

The two museum exhibits educated both residents in and outside of the Rapp Road community. Residents in the Rapp Road Community were taught that everyday objects have the power to tell the story of the people who use them. For example, after the Tapestry of Albany County opening, Javan Owens stopped by Dickson's house to see if the museum wanted to use his father's hand plow in the exhibit. Owens was convinced that the old rusty plow was of no use. When Owens realized that the hand plow demonstrated how the people on Rapp Road tilled their fields and used their land was a part of their community's history and personal identity, he told Dickson he would go back and look around his garage for other objects. Rapp Road residents began to look at objects in their attics and garages with a new eye. Another interesting object that Rapp Road resident Girlie Ferguson donated was a bleached flour sack. Ferguson said that the flour sack belonged to her grandmother, who as a sharecropper in Shubuta bleached the flour logo out of the cotton sack so she could use the material to make clothes.

These exhibits also taught people outside of the community the value of public history; the idea that the little-known Rapp Road community became a New York State and National Historic District sent a message to the general public that community history is important and should be documented for future generations. People began to ask themselves that if this small community in the middle of the Pine Bush could be important, why can't our community be important too? The publicity around the Rapp Road community is good for the Albany area, as well as New York State, particularly for other African American communities. Until then many of the African American communities in the Albany area were ignored or misrepresented.

The historical momentum surrounding the community continued and in September 2006 the New York State Education Department chartered the Rapp Road Historical Association (RRHA). This association, consisting of a Board of Trustees from both inside and outside the community, is charged with preserving the history of the Rapp Road community. In its first year, RRHA was responsible for sponsoring several lectures, an exhibit, and a walking tour of the Rapp Road Historic District.

Historical applications and practices gave the Rapp Road community a tool for preserving its past. In addition to Rapp Road's history as a significant addition to the base of historical knowledge, Emma Dickson has made sure that the Rapp Road story continues for future generations. In an interview she said, "We started very early on with making sure grandchildren, cousins, nieces, nephews—that they know the story and how important it is to maintain. My kids have been told that I will come back and haunt them to their deaths if they don't try to keep everything in place, which might even be more difficult in years to come than it was for me."[56]

CONCLUSION

Looking Back at the Rapp Road Experience

A major theme running through all of the oral history interviews conducted was faith in God. Religion was the one common denominator among the migrants and their families who settled on Rapp Road. For many of the original landowners, Louis Parson was their preacher in Mississippi, the person responsible for driving them or their family members to Albany for the opportunity of a better life, and the person who helped them adjust to northern urban living. Upon arrival in Albany most of the Mississippi migrants joined Parson's church, the First Church of God in Christ. Through the church, Parson and fellow church members were able to provide for and aid newly arrived migrants from the South. When Parson bought the land on Rapp Road, he only sold it to church members, thus making it a closed community. This closed community status, along with the fundamental nature of Pentecostal religion, and the striking resemblance to the rural South reinforced the idea that the Rapp Road community was indeed *their* "Promised Land." An example of how religion played such a big part of the Rapp Road community's life is that the original landowners named the area the "Holy Land" because of the entire community's strong religious faith. Also, community members firmly believed that God led Parson to Albany. Parson was viewed as a modern day Moses, leading his people to a better life.

Another common characteristic throughout the interviews was that the Rapp Road residents and their family members felt they had two homes. Their first home was in the South, and in a majority of the cases, home was Shubuta. This first home, although plagued with discrimination and violence toward their fellow African Americans, was cherished and visited often. Their second home was on Rapp Road. Residents were able to buy land and build their own home for the first time in their lives. The gardens they kept were their own and they could reap all the benefits of their hard work. It is telling that these first-generation residents recreated their southern life on Rapp Road. These transplanted southerners were able to bring the good things about the South to Albany, and because Rapp Road was basically a closed community, residents were able to keep discrimination and violence away from their home life.

Second-generation Rapp Road members revere the South, but not as deeply as their parents. For many, the South was only their home for a short time. The South was the place they visited to see older relatives and attend homecoming reunions. This generation heard more stories about southern discrimination and violence toward blacks than actually being victims of that hatred. The second generation of Rapp Road residents grew up there, moved away, and then returned to raise their own families there. The original landowners had the task of clearing the Pine Bush land and making it into the "Promised Land," while the second generation had the duty of saving and preserving it from encroaching commercial development, and passing on the community's traditions, stories, and history.

The saving of the Rapp Road community became possible because members turned to historical preservation as a tool. Historic preservation offered the community many different avenues of defense, which, in this case, were made possible by "town and gown" cooperation. "Town and gown" refers to the relationship between members of the city (town) and members of the university (gown). In the spirit of "town and gown" many college-level history students learn from institutions and groups in their school's community. The greater benefits from "town and gown" relationships usually come from public historians rather than academic historians. Although both types of historians want to add to the body of historical knowledge, the end product of the academic historian is a published article or monograph based on his or her research. The public historian, on the other hand, wants to produce solid academic research, but also wants to actively engage the community in the preservation, interpretation, and promotion of their research. This process goes beyond the written word and is manifested in such ways as exhibits, tours, lectures, reenactments, and web pages.

Ultimately, Louis W. Parson created an outlet for a southern lifestyle in a northern city. With the help of local public historians and the hard work of dedicated community members the Rapp Road community continues to thrive and prosper. In August 2007 the community celebrated its fiftieth family reunion. Friends and family from across the country traveled to Rapp Road to mark this historic event. The highlight of the weekend-long celebration was the family reunion picnic attended by more than 300. The day began with Sunday morning worship services at Wilborn Temple First Church of God in Christ followed by an afternoon picnic on Rapp Road. This important anniversary marked a milestone for several of the residents—they were still here despite all of the challenges, sacrifices, and hard times. This community serves as a testimony to the hard work, faith, and values of a group of Americans who looked for a new life—and found it in the Pine Bush of Albany, New York.

Appendixes

Map of the United States

WPA Photographs of
Mississippi, circa 1930

"These cotton hoers work from 6 a.m. to 7 p.m. for $1, near Clarksdale, Mississippi," photograph courtesy of Mississippi Department of Archives and History, PI.1986.0026.86

"Cabin Interior," by Marion Post Wolcott, photograph courtesy of Mississippi Department of Archives and History, PI.1986.0026.210

"School Interior, Mileston Mississippi," by Marion Post Wolcott, photograph courtesy of Mississippi Department of Archives and History, PI.1986.0026.163

"Moving Highway 1, Washington County," by Dorothea Lange, photograph courtesy of Mississippi Department of Archives and History, PI.1986.0026.85

APPENDIX 3

Shubuta, Mississippi, African American Head of Household
Occupational Percentages, 1930

		Frequency	Percent	Valid Percent	Cumulative Percent
Valid	laborer	88	34.4	36.5	36.5
	farmer	86	33.6	35.7	72.2
	cleaner	1	.4	.4	72.6
	cook	11	4.3	4.6	77.2
	laundry	11	4.3	4.6	81.7
	preacher	8	3.1	3.3	85.1
	odd jobs	1	.4	.4	85.5
	log sawer	3	1.2	1.2	86.7
	carpenter	4	1.6	1.7	88.4
	janitor	1	.4	.4	88.8
	delivery	1	.4	.4	89.2
	servant	4	1.6	1.7	90.9
	edgerman	4	1.6	1.7	92.5
	teamster	2	.8	.8	93.4
	blacksmith	1	.4	.4	93.8
	chopper	5	2.0	2.1	95.9
	agent	2	.8	.8	96.7
	truck driver	3	1.2	1.2	97.9
	plastering	1	.4	.4	98.3
	brick mason	1	.4	.4	98.8
	grader	1	.4	.4	99.2
	school	1	.4	.4	99.6
	logger	1	.4	.4	100.0
	Total	241	94.1	100.0	
Missing	99	15	5.9		
Total		256	100.0		

Source: United States Bureau of the Census, *Fifteenth Census of the United States Taken in 1930* (Washington, D.C.: Government Printing Office, 1932)

Detail of Albany Ward Map, 1930

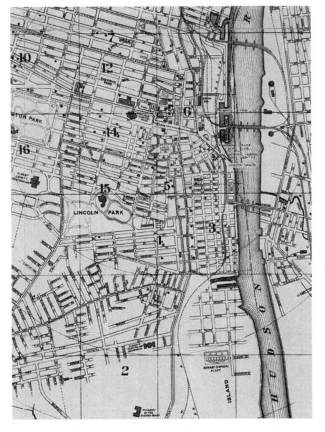

Source: Albany and Rensselaer, N.Y. Directory, 1930–1958 (Albany, N.Y.: Sampson and Murdock Company)

APPENDIX 5

Abridged List of African American Housing Conditions in Albany, New York, circa 1928

The State of Repair in these houses can only be arbitrarily measured. The best index is obtained from some of the particular families covered. The conditions in these families represent some of the most flagrant discomforts in the Negro homes:

Family #6: Woman works for sporting girls. House was damaged by fire and never restored.

Family #15: Roof leaks continually. Family of 6. Toilet is on the back porch. Back yard very dirty.

Family #29: Toilet outside and out of order. Landlord will not fix. Ceiling down. Doors don't shut. Kitchen always cold.

Family #45: Very damp. Floor and ceiling in poor conditions.

Family #93: House very unsanitary. Water stands in yard constantly. Outside toilet.

Family #96: Two windowless bedrooms.

Family #113: In Albany ten weeks. $25.00 for 5 rooms, no bath. House is cold, walls very dirty, all in need of papering.

Family #157: Rooms dark, smoky and ill-kept. Toilet freezes, unclean, bad odors.

Family #164: Man lives alone, 2 rooms, $13.00 per month. Repairs never made. A common toilet in hall which he refuses to use. Closes shutters on the front of the house to keep warm. At time of visit was huddled over oil lamp. Rooms very unclean.

Family #200: Family of eight. Six children under 12. House in alley. Outside toilet. Four rooms. Rent $15 a month.

Family #213: Entrance to toilet through kitchen. Toilet is without door. Rent is $20 for five rooms.

Family #234: Occupied house for seven years. Landlord refuses to do any repairing. Tenant has put in electricity, papered and painted rooms—repaired two floors—yet, rent was raised from $17 to $20.

Source: National Urban League, Department of Research and Investigation, *The Negro Population—Albany, New York* (New York: National Urban League, 1928), 11–13.

Rent Charges for African American Housing in Albany, New York, circa 1928

A pertinent factor related to this lack of convenience is the amount of rent paid. The Negro population being limited in its housing by certain areas as well as houses, is forced to pay the price demanded for the restricted supply.

The largest group of families paid $15 to $19 a month for rent and the second largest paid $20 to $24 monthly. Fifty-five per cent of all renters paid $20.00 or more for rent.

The four room dwelling was the most common and showed the greatest variation in the amount of rental paid. From $8 to $36 was paid for these four room dwellings.

The wide variation in rentals is due to several factors among which may be mentioned:

1—The inadequacies, varying lack of conveniences, repairs and sanitation in sixty-three per cent of the houses;

2—The increases in rentals due to the installation of electricity and bathrooms, or painting and plastering;

3—The extent to which families occupy one floor of four or five rooms in three and four story houses.

The average monthly rental for houses by number of rooms occupied by Negroes was:

Dwellings of 1 room.....$5.00   Dwellings of 6 rooms....$25.11

Dwellings of 2 rooms...$11.17   Dwellings of 7 rooms....$30.41

Dwellings of 3 rooms...$12.43   Dwellings of 8 rooms....$37.99

Dwellings of 4 rooms...$17.61   Dwellings of 9 rooms....$43.00

Dwellings of 5 rooms...$22.14   Dwellings of 10 rooms...$50.00

Compared with rents per room per month for a group of cities the Albany Negro pays a somewhat smaller rental than larger and more congested cities of the North.

Source: National Urban League, Department of Research and Investigation, *The Negro Population—Albany, New York* (New York: National Urban League, 1928), 13–14.

APPENDIX 7

Photographs of Albany's South End, circa 1940

"Dongan Avenue [At Bleecker Street]," courtesy of the Morris Gerber Photograph Collection, Albany Institute of History and Art, 1993.010.694.1P

"Franklin and Herkimer," courtesy of the Morris Gerber Photograph Collection, Albany Institute of History and Art, 1993.010.858.1P

Photographs of Rapp Road Community Members

Louis W. Parson, photograph courtesy of Emma Dickson

Alfred and Leola Woodard,
Hattiesburg, Mississippi, circa
1933, photograph courtesy of
Emma Dickson

The Franklin family, circa 1955. The Franklins moved to Albany in 1936
from Chicora, Mississippi.
(Top row L-R) Louise, Louis, Robert, Doll, Clarence, Elsie
(Bottom row L-R) Alma, Luella, Sam, Sarah
Photograph courtesy of Rhonda Norman

I'm

I

Nora Lee McCann on Rapp Road, August 1955, photograph courtesy of Ann Stanfield

(L-R) Oseana Woodard, Bertha McCann (baby), and Naomi McCann on Rapp Road, August 1955, photograph courtesy of Ann Stanfield

(L-R) Girlie Ferguson, Emma Dickson, Lucy Johnson Oakley in Mobile, Alabama, November 2002, photograph by author

List of Original Landowners and Purchase Dates of Land on Rapp Road, Albany, New York

Samuel Coleman—January 27, 1942

Esco Nelson—November 9, 1942

Joshua Burney—August 24, 1943; October 15, 1945

Butler Corley—August 25, 1943; January 4, 1956

Sam Franklin—September 29, 1943

Daniel McCann—March 10, 1944

Clarence Jackson—March 19, 1945

Javan Owens—March 28, 1945

Abbie Johnson—May 11, 1945

Walter H. Woods—June 20, 1945

Daisy Kimball—August 11, 1943

Jesse C. Harmon—February 24, 1944

William McCann and Wife [Tempie]—July 17, 1944; May 25, 1950; July 17, 1950

Labor Johnson—August 31, 1944; October 15, 1962

Theodore Woodard—August 31, 1944

Benjamin Nixon—August 31, 1944

Caesar Moore—August 31, 1944

Alfred Woodard—July 8, 1946

Luella Franklin—January 24, 1953

Jessie Garrett and Wife [Melinda]—January 4, 1956

Libbie Toliver—April 3, 1958

William Wilborn—October 17, 1958

Sammie Fantroy and Wife [Henrietta]—October 3, 1962;
    September 5, 1963

Source: Accession Land Deeds located at the Albany County Clerk Office, Albany, New York

Photographs of Rapp Road Houses, circa 1990

5 Rapp Road, originally owned by Javan Owens, Sr., photograph courtesy of the City Neighbors Collection, Albany Institute of History & Art

8 Rapp Road, originally owned by William and Libbie Toliver, photograph courtesy of the Albany Institute of History & Art

14 Rapp Road, originally
owned by Samuel
and Isabel Coleman,
photograph courtesy of
the Albany Institute
of History & Art

22 Rapp Road,
originally owned by
Alfred and Leola
Woodard, photograph
courtesy of the Albany
Institute of History
& Art

23 Rapp Road,
originally owned by
Willie and Tempie
McCann, photograph
courtesy of the Albany
Institute of History
& Art

29 Rapp Road,
originally owned by
Willie McCann,
photograph courtesy
of the Albany Institute
of History & Art

31 Rapp Road,
originally owned
by Albert and Susie
Farley, photograph
courtesy of the Albany
Institute of
History & Art

39 Rapp Road,
originally owned
by Labor and Clara
Johnson, photograph
courtesy of the
Albany Institute
of History & Art

50 Rapp Road, originally owned by Jessie and Melinda Garrett, photograph courtesy of the Albany Institute of History & Art

54 Rapp Road, originally owned by Butler and Effie Corley, photograph courtesy of the Albany Institute of History & Art

59 Rapp Road, originally owned by Charles Smith, then Louis and Frances Parson, photograph courtesy of the Albany Institute of History & Art

67 Rapp Road, originally owned by Sammie and Henrietta Fantroy, photograph courtesy of the Albany Institute of History & Art

69 Rapp Road, originally owned by James Hunt, photograph courtesy of the Albany Institute of History & Art

Smokehouse used for annual reunion, located at 38 Rapp Road, built by Daniel McCann, photograph courtesy of the Albany Institute of History & Art

APPENDIX 11

Photographs of Fields
on Rapp Road

McCann Field, circa 1990, photograph courtesy of the Albany Institute of History & Art

Fields on Rapp Road, circa 1990, photograph courtesy of Albany Institute of History & Art

Comparison Photographs of Shubuta and Rapp Road

Baptism in river, Mississippi, circa 1935, photograph courtesy of Mississippi Department of Archives and History, PI/WPA/Negroes

Dr. William Wilborn performing baptism for the First Church of God in Christ members on the Rensselaer side of the Hudson River, circa 1955, photograph courtesy of Ann Stanfield

Homes in Shubuta, Mississippi, 2002, photograph by author

Ressy McCann's house in Shubuta, Mississippi, 2002, photograph by author

Road in Shubuta, Mississippi, photograph by author

Old Rapp Road,
circa 1990,
photograph courtesy
of Albany Institute
of History & Art

Fields in Shubuta,
photograph by
author

Fields on Rapp
Road, circa 1990,
photograph courtesy
of Albany Institute
of History & Art

APPENDIX 13

Maps on and around
the Rapp Road Community

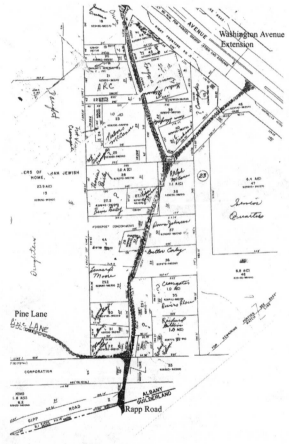

Albany County assessment map of Rapp Road area, circa 1997

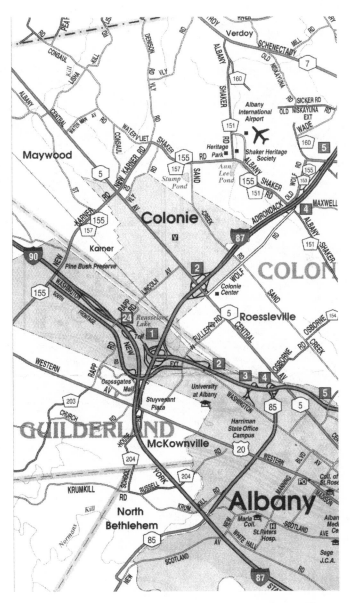

Map of Rapp Road area, circa 1995, courtesy of New York State Albany
Heritage

Aerial view of Rapp Road Historic District, 2004, courtesy of New York
State Historic Preservation Bureau

Notes

INTRODUCTION

1. Peter Gottlieb, *Making Their Own Way: Southern Blacks' Migration to Pittsburgh, 1916–30* (Chicago: University of Illinois Press, 1987), 14.

2. Ibid., 15.

3. Eddie McDonald, interview by author, mini-disk recording, Shubuta, Mississippi, 11 November 2002.

4. Carole Marks, *Farewell—We're Good and Gone: The Great Black Migration* (Indianapolis: Indiana University Press, 1989), 141.

5. James Grossman, *Land of Hope: Chicago, Black Southerners, and the Great Migration* (Chicago: University of Chicago Press, 1989), 34.

6. Ronald L. F. Davis, "Creating Jim Crow: In-Depth Essay," in The History of Jim Crow website [database online] (Public Broadcasting Station: accessed 15 January 2003); available from http://www.jimcrow history.org.

7. Philip Koslow, ed., *The New York Public Library African American Desk Reference* (New York: Stonesong Press, 1999), 316.

8. Ibid.

9. Grossman, *Land of Hope*, 27.

10. "Cook the books" is a phrase used by the Woodard family when they talked about sharecrop farming in Shubuta, Mississippi. It meant that the accounts were altered. Alfred Woodard was a victim of a dishonest plantation owner who said he owed more money than he did. Emma Dickson, interview by author, tape recording, Albany, New York, 19 April 2000.

11. Grossman, *Land of Hope*, 27.

12. Ibid., 93.

13. Milton Sernett, *Bound for the Promised Land: African American Religion and the Great Migration* (Durham: Duke University Press, 1997), 96–98.

14. Grossman, *Land of Hope*, 128.

15. Ibid., 46.

16. Ibid.

17. Ibid., 28–29.

18. Ibid., 29.

CHAPTER 1. SHUBUTA, MISSISSIPPI

1. "Negroes Should Remain in South," *Shubuta Mississippi Messenger*, 5 September 1919.

2. Ibid.

3. Jerry D. Mason, *Shubuta, Mississippi: Home of the Red Artesian Well* (Shubuta: author, 2001), 6.

4. Clarke County Chamber of Commerce, *Historic Clarke County* (Quitman, Mississippi: privately printed, n.d.), 20.

5. Ibid.

6. Ibid, 6.

7. Gradie Pearl Dansby, *Historic Clarke County* (Quitman, Mississippi: privately printed, 1996), 16.

8. United States Bureau of the Census, *Populations by Counties and Minor Civil Divisions 1920, 1910, 1900, and 1890* (Washington, D.C.: Government Printing Office, 1921).

9. Mason, *Shubuta, Mississippi*, 7.

10. All statistics in this section are taken from: United States Bureau of the Census, *Fifteenth Census of the United States Taken in 1930*, Clarke County, Shubuta, Mississippi.

11. *Fifteenth Census of the United States*.

12. Herbert Gutman, *The Black Family in Slavery and Freedom, 1750–1925* (New York: Vintage Books, 1976), 448.

13. Household classifications adopted from Herbert Gutman's *The Black Family in Slavery and Freedom, 1750—1925*; Tamara Hareven,

Family Time and Industrial Time: The Relationship between the Family and Work in a New England Industrial Community (Cambridge: Cambridge University Press, 1982).

14. Gutman, *Black Family*, 448–49.

15. Ibid., 445.

16. *Fifteenth Census of the United States*, Shubuta, Mississippi.

17. Ibid.

18. Ada Wells and Irene Doherty, *Historic Research Project: Wayne County, Mississippi* (Washington, D.C.: Federal Writers Project, 1937), chapter 13.

19. E. Franklin Frazier, *The Negro Church in America* (New York: Schocken Books, 1964), 51.

20. I use the word "official" here because it was possible that black people gathered together to celebrate their religion in private homes and areas unknown to the general public.

21. Willis McDonald, interview by author, mini-disk recording, Shubuta, Mississippi, 11 November 2002.

22. Alma McDonald, interview by author, mini-disk recording, Shubuta, Mississippi, 11 November 2002.

23. Rhonda Norman, interview by author, written responses via email, Albany, New York, 14 April 2004.

24. Booker T. Washington and W. E. B. Du Bois, *The Negro in the South: His Economic Progress in Relation to His Moral and Religious Development* (Philadelphia: G. W. Jacobs, 1917), 176.

25. Milton Sernett, *Bound for the Promised Land: African American Religion and the Great Migration* (Durham: Duke University Press, 1997), 35.

26. *Fifteenth Census of the United States*, Shubuta, Mississippi.

27. Mississippi Department of Education, *African American Education Folder*, Record 50, Jackson, Mississippi: Mississippi Department of Archives and History.

28. Ibid.

29. Eva Haney and Anna B. Hardee, "Historic Clarke County, Mississippi, Assignment #26 (Washington, D.C.: Federal Writers Project, 1936).

30. Mason, *Shubuta, Mississippi*, 43.

31. Haney and Hardee, "Assignment #26."

32. Ibid.

33. Mason, *Shubuta, Mississippi*, 43.

34. Diane Granat, "Saving the Rosenwald Schools: Preserving African American History" [database online] (Alicia Patterson Foundation, accessed 28 February 2003); available from http://www.aliciapatterson.org/APF2004/Granat/Granat.html

35. Eva Haney and Anna B. Hardee, "Historic Clarke County, Mississippi," Assignments #19, 57 (Washington, D.C.: Federal Writers Project, 1936).

36. Ibid.

37. Girlie Ferguson, interview by author, tape recording, East Nassau, New York, 15 April 2000.

38. Ibid.

39. *Fifteenth Census of the United States*, Shubuta, Mississippi.

40. Ibid.

41. Haney and Hardee, "Assignment #19."

42. W. E. B. Du Bois, *The Souls of Black Folk* (Chicago: A.C. McClurg and Company, 1903), 151.

43. Ferguson interview.

44. Vernon Lane Wharton, *The Negro in Mississippi, 1865–1890* (New York: Harper Torchbooks, 1965), 62.

45. Ferguson interview.

46. Ibid.

47. Fred Thomas, interview by Emma Dickson and author, mini-disk recording, Shubuta, Mississippi, 12 November 2002.

48. Geneva Conway, "A Capital Area Oral History," public program recorded on tape, Albany Institute of History and Art, 22 February 1997.

49. Eddie Johnson Burton, interview by author, mini-disk recording, Waynesboro, Mississippi, 14 November 2002.

50. Ibid.

51. Mason, *Shubuta, Mississippi*, 17.

52. Ibid.

53. *Fifteenth Census of the United States*, Shubuta, Mississippi.

54. Ibid.

55. Wells and Doherty, *Historic Research Project*, chapter 13.

56. Ibid.

57. Wells and Doherty, *Historic Research Project*, chapter 13.

58. Ferguson interview.

59. Burton interview.

60. Haney and Hardee, "Assignment #10."

61. Grossman, *Land of Hope*, 29.

62. *Shubuta Mississippi Messenger*, 5 June 1914.

63. *Shubuta Mississippi Messenger*, 17 December 1915.

64. "Weevil Effects Showing Strong," *Shubuta Mississippi Messenger*, 21 December 1923.

65. Grossman, *Land of Hope*, 29.

66. Du Bois, *Souls of Black Folk*, 89.

67. Mason, *Shubuta, Mississippi*, 40.

68. Ferguson interview.

69. Eddie McDonald, interview by author, mini-disk recording, Shubuta, Mississippi, 12 November 2002.

70. Ibid.

71. Ibid.

72. Wells and Doherty, "Assignment #22."

73. Eddie McDonald interview.

74. McKinley Johnson, interview by author, mini-disk recording, Albany, New York, 24 February 2004.

75. Ibid.

76. *Shubuta Mississippi Messenger*, 16 December 1921.

77. Philip Koslow, ed., *The New York Public Library African American Desk Reference* (New York: Stonesong Press, 1999), 316.

78. "Shubuta Lynchings," *The Cincinnati Union*, 31 May 1919, Ohio Historical Archives, Newspaper Roll #8847, Vol. 13, No. 22, page:01 accessed at: http://dbs.ohiohistory.org/africanam/page.cfm?ID=760&Current=01_01A

79. Mason, *Shubuta, Mississippi*, 103.

80. Ibid.

CHAPTER 2. "GOD LED ME TO ALBANY"

1. United States Bureau of the Census, *Fifteenth Census of the United States Taken in 1930*, Albany County, Albany, New York, Wards 1–19, New York State Library, Albany, New York.

2. Ibid.

3. John J. McEneny, *Albany: Capital City on the Hudson* (Sun Valley, California: American Historical Press, 1998), 79–81.

4. Ibid.

5. Ibid.

6. Ibid., 79–81.

7. Ibid, 151–53.

8. William Kennedy, *O Albany! Improbable City of Political Wizards, Fearless Ethnics, Spectacular Aristocrats, Splendid Nobodies, and Underrated Scoundrels* (New York: The Viking Press, 1983), 258–59.

9. *Fifteenth Census of the United States*, Albany, New York.

10. M. C. Lawton 75th Anniversary Celebration Pamphlet, M. C. Lawton Club Collection, M. E. Grenander Department of Special Collections and Archives, University at Albany.

11. Ibid.

12. Harold Winchester, "The Early History of the Albany Inter-Racial Council," The Ruth Robert African Americans in Albany Collection at the Albany Institute of History and Art, Albany, New York.

13. Ibid.

14. Ibid.

15. National Urban League, Department of Research and Investigation, *The Negro Population—Albany, New York* (New York: National Urban League, 1928), 41.

16. Winchester, "Early History."

17. NAACP Albany Branch, "A Brief History Albany Branch," 50th Anniversary Freedom Fund Dinner booklet, 8 November 1985, University at Albany Library, M. E. Grenander Department of Special Collections and Archives, NAACP—Albany, NY, Branch Records, 1966–68 Series 1: Subject Files History Box 3, Folder 4.

18. The Scottsboro Boys were nine black teenagers involved in a two-decade court battle beginning in 1931 against execution for the alleged rape of two white girls.

19. NAACP Albany, 50th Anniversary Freedom Fund Dinner booklet.

20. Kennedy, *O Albany!*, 257–58.

21. Ferguson interview.

22. *Fifteenth Census of the United States*, Albany, New York.

23. Ibid.

24. Bill Kennedy, "New South End Emerging amid Urban, Social Progress," *Albany Times Union*, 13 or March 1967.

25. Ibid.

26. Conway interview.

27. Kennedy, *O Albany!*, 157.

28. National Urban League, *Negro Population*, 10.

29. Ibid.

30. Ibid.

31. Ibid.

32. Geneva Conway and Leon Dukes, "A Capital Area Oral History," public program recorded on tape, Albany Institute of History and Art, 22 February 1997.

33. Patricia Beebee, "A Capital Area Oral History," public program recorded on tape, Albany Institute of History and Art, 22 February 1997.

34. James Stamper, "A Capital Area Oral History," public program recorded on tape, Albany Institute of History and Art, 22 February 1997.

35. Ibid.

36. Dukes interview.

37. *Albany Times Union*, 15 December 1981, clipping file, NAACP—Albany, NY Branch Records, 1966–68 Series 1: Subject Files History Box 3, Folder 4, University at Albany Library, M. E. Grenander Department of Special Collections and Archives.

38. Ibid.

39. Ibid.

40. Ibid.

41. McKinley Johnson interview.

42. Ibid.

43. Ibid.

44. Grossman, *Lord of Hope*, 91.

45. *Fifteenth Census of the United States*, Albany, New York.

46. Program of the Albany Inter-Racial Council, 1929, M. C. Lawton Club papers, M. E. Grenander Department of Special Collections and Archives, University at Albany.

47. M. C. Lawton Presidential Report, July 1928, M. C. Lawton Club papers, M. E. Grenander Department of Special Collections and Archives, University at Albany.

48. Ibid., 5.

49. Ibid., 6.

50. *Fifteenth Census of the United States*, Albany, New York.

51. 12th through 18th United States Census, Albany, N.Y.

52. National Urban League, *Negro Population*, 7.

53. Ibid., 25.

54. Ibid., 2.

55. McEneny, *Albany*, 27.

56. Kennedy, "New South End Emerging."

57. McEneny, *Albany*, 27.

58. *Fifteenth Census of the United States*, Albany, New York.

59. Ibid.

60. Ibid.

61. Ibid.

62. Ibid.

63. National Urban League, *Negro Population*, 9.

64. Stamper interview.

65. Ibid.

66. Ibid.

67. The Holland Tunnel connects New York and New Jersey under the Hudson River. Construction began in 1920 and ended in 1927. The Holland Tunnel was the world's first long, underwater, mechanically ventilated vehicular tunnel.

68. Dukes interview.

69. Ibid.

70. Ibid.

71. Ibid.

72. Conway interview.

73. *Fifteenth Census of the United States*, Albany, New York.

74. Rose Juan Jackson, "The Black Educational Experience in a Northern City: Albany, New York, 1830–1970" (PhD diss., Northwestern University, 1976), 139.

75. National Urban League, *Negro Population*, 39.

76. Ibid., 35.

77. Ibid., 34.

78. Ibid., 35.

79. M. C. Lawton Report, 11.

80. Ibid., 12.

81. Conway interview.

82. M. C. Lawton Report, 10.

83. Ibid.

84. Stamper interview.

85. Conway interview.

86. Ibid.

87. According to the National Urban League survey the total number of African Americans affiliated with white churches in Albany, New York, was less than fifty. Black church members were associated with Catholic, Episcopal, Presbyterian, Reformed, Baptist, and Methodist denominations.

88. National Urban League, *Negro Population*, 38.

89. Ibid.

90. Ibid.

91. Ibid.

92. Bill Kennedy, "New South End Emerging."

93. Sernett, *Bound for the Promised Land*, 188.

94. Ibid.

95. Seth M. Scheiner, "The Negro Church and the Northern City," in *Seven on Black: Reflections on the Negro Experience in America*, edited by William Shade and Roy Herrenkohl (Philadelphia: J. B. Lippincott Company, 1969), 103.

96. MC Lawton Report 7 July 1930, M. C. Lawton papers, M. E. Grenander Department of Special Collections and Archives, University at Albany.

97. *Wilborn Temple 75 Years of Love in the Making, 1927–2002* (Albany: Wilborn Temple First Church of God in Christ, 2002).

98. Ibid.

99. Orlean Rucker, interview by author, tape recording, Albany, New York, 19 April 2000.

100. *Wilborn Temple 75 Years.*

101. Rucker interview.

102. Ibid.

103. Ibid.

104. Ibid.

105. Emma Dickson, interview by author, written notes, Albany, New York, 17 May 2004.

106. Grossman, *Land of Hope*, 94.

107. Dickson interview, 17 May 2004.

108. Norman interview.

109. Ibid.

110. Although I can find no formal record of Parson's arrest or any type of police action against him, several oral history interviews state that the Albany City police issued him a court summons for bringing black people to Albany. One possible explanation is that the police were harassing Parson because he was bringing poor blacks to Albany to live. This police harassment would explain why when Frances Parson went to court her husband's name was never called as explained further on in this chapter.

111. Rucker interview.

112. Ibid.

113. McKinley Johnson interview.

114. Emma Dickson, interview by author, tape recording, Albany, New York, 16 April 2000.

115. Christopher Ringwald, "Students Take Trek Through Black Church," *Albany Times Union*, 13 July 1997.

116. Ibid.

117. Ibid.

118. McKinley Johnson interview.

119. Nora Lee McCann, public comment at "An Evening with Emma," tape recording, Wilborn Temple, Albany, New York, 22 February 2002.

120. Dickson interview, 16 April 2000.

121. Ferguson interview.

122. Henrietta and Sammie Fantroy, interview by author, tape recording, Albany, New York, 19 April 2000.

123. Ibid.

124. Ibid.

125. *Wilborn Temple 75 Years.*

126. Ibid.

127. Ferguson interview.

128. Sarah McCann obituary, *Albany Times Union*, 16 October 1995.

129. Juanita Nabors, interview by author, tape recording, Albany, New York, 17 April 2000.

130. Ibid.

131. Fantroy interview.

132. *Albany and Rensselaer, N.Y. Directory, 1930–1958* (Albany, New York: Sampson and Murdock Company).

133. Conway interview.

134. Sernett, *Bound for the Promised Land*, 96–98; "What We Believe" [database online] (First Church of God in Christ official website, accessed 30 July 2004), http://www.cogic.com

135. Ibid.

136. Kennedy, *O Albany!*, 156.

137. Bill Kennedy, "New South End Emerging."

138. Ibid.

139. Ferguson interview.

140. Conway interview.

CHAPTER 3. "WHATEVER WE NEEDED, HE COULD GET IT"

1. Emma Dickson, "The Promised Land: From Mississippi to the South End to Rapp Road," public lecture, W. S. Hackett Middle School, Albany, New York, 3 February 2000.

2. Land Accession Deed, 2 May 1930, Albany County Clerk's Office.

3. Ibid.

4. Ibid.

5. C. R. Rosenberry, "Thruway May Reopen Pine Bush," *Albany Times Union*, 19 November 1950.

6. Rucker interview.

7. Catherine Clabby, "A Promised Land That Kept Its Word," *Albany Times Union*, 19 August 1990.

8. Ralph McCann, interview by author, tape recording, Albany, New York, 19 April 2000.

9. Nabors interview.

10. Emma Dickson, interview by author, phone interview, Albany, New York, 1 December 2003.

11. Ferguson interview.

12. Rucker interview.

13. Ibid.

14. *Wilborn Temple 75 Years.*

15. Ibid.

16. McKinley Johnson interview.

17. Dickson, "Promised Land."

18. Dickson interview, 16 April 2000.

19. Nabors interview.

20. Fantroy interview.

21. Dickson interview, 16 April 2000.

22. Ibid.

23. Ibid.

24. Dickson interview, 16 November 2003.

25. Ibid.

26. Ralph McCann interview.

27. McKinley Johnson interview.

28. Ibid.

29. Dickson interview, 16 November 2003.

30. Ibid.

31. Ibid.

32. Ibid.

33. Ibid.

34. Ibid. Mother Burney's house sat along with three other homes on the present-day site of Home Depot.

35. Ibid.

36. Ibid.

37. Rucker interview.

38. Dickson, "Promised Land."

39. *Wilborn Temple 75 Years.*

40. Ibid.

41. Ibid.

42. Dickson interview, 16 November 2003.

43. Ibid.

44. Emma Dickson, interview by author, phone interview, Albany, New York, 1 December 2003.

45. Gottlieb, *Making Their Own Way*, 20.

46. Ibid., 21.

47. Alma MacDonald interview.

48. Dickson interview, 16 April 2000.

49. Ibid.

50. Don Rittner, *Pine Bush: Albany's Last Frontier* (Albany, New York: Pine Bush Historic Preservation Project, 1976), xvii.

51. Dickson interview.

52. *Wilborn Temple 75 Years*; Ralph McCann interview.

53. Rachel Carley, *The Visual Dictionary of American Domestic Architecture* (New York: Henry Holt and Company, 1994), 116.

54. Virginia McAlestar and Lee McAlestar, *A Field Guide to American Houses* (New York: Alfred A. Knopf, 2000), 100–01.

55. Grossman, *Making Their Own Way*, 99.

56. *Fourteenth Census of the United States*, Albany, New York; *Fifteenth Census of the United States*, Albany, New York.

CHAPTER 4. CHANGE COMES TO RAPP ROAD

1. Clemmie Harris, "Suburban Populism: A Short History on Environmental Politics in the Pine Bush Region from 1950–1982" (master's thesis, University at Albany, 2002), 3.

2. Harris, "Suburban Populism," 4.

3. Ibid.

4. Ibid., 5.

5. C. R. Rosenberry, "Thruway May Reopen Pine Bush," *Albany Times Union*, 19 November 1950.

6. Ibid.

7. "Development of City's Pine Bush Area Gives Planners a Golden Opportunity," *Albany Knickerbocker News*, 9 July 1960.

8. Jeff Coplon, "How to Make $1 Million in the Pine Bush," *Albany Knickerbocker News*, 14 March 1978.

9. Ibid.

10. Ibid.

11. Dickson interview, 16 April 2000.

12. Edward Carey, "Blacks Fear Crossgates Mall Will Mean Change for 'Holy Land,'" *Albany Knickerbocker News*, 21 July 1981.

13. Emma Dickson, interview by author, written notes, Albany, New York, 16 January 2004.

14. Ibid.

15. Carey, "Blacks Fear Crossgates Mall."

16. Ibid.

17. Ibid.

18. Harris, "Suburban Populism," 51.

19. Ibid., 50.

20. Ibid., 51.

21. Carey, "Blacks Fear Crossgates Mall."

22. Dickson interview, 16 April 2000.

23. Ibid.

24. Tim Schick, "Vocal Crowd Divided in Views on Crossgates," *Albany Times Union*, 30 July 1981.

25. Ibid.

26. Ibid.

27. Ibid.

28. Ibid.

29. Ibid.

30. Town of Guilderland Zoning Board of Appeals, "Pyramid Crossgates Public Hearing," 29 July 1981, Guilderland Town Hall, Guilderland, New York.

31. Town of Guilderland Zoning Board of Appeals, "Pyramid Crossgates Public Hearing," 26 August 1981, Guilderland Town Hall, Guilderland, New York.

32. Carey, "Blacks Fear Crossgates Mall."

33. Frank Commisso, interview with author, mini-disk recording, Albany, New York, 2 February 2004.

34. Dickson interview, 16 January 2004.

35. Von Jones and Ellen Pearlmutter, "No Hydrants, They're at Fire's Mercy," *Albany Times Union*, 9 April 1981.

36. Dickson interview, 16 January 2004.

37. Superintendent Building Department City of Albany, "Letter to Mayor Erastus Corning," Albany County Hall of Records, Corning Papers, Box 229, Folder 32/3/15–17.

38. Ibid.

39. John Dieffenbach, "Residents Decry Plans for Rapp Road," *Albany Knickerbocker News*, 22 June 1987.

40. Ibid.

41. Ibid.

42. Ibid.

43. Aisling Swift, "Crossgates Commons Increases Building Loan to $22.3 Million," *Albany Times Union*, 6 October 1994.

44. Dickson interview, 16 April 2000.

45. Ibid.

46. Jay Jochnowitz, "NiMo Hands Residents a Victory by Altering Plans for a Substation," *Albany Times Union*, 9 May 1994.

47. Ibid.

48. Ibid.

49. "Crossgates Expansion Work to Start," *Albany Times Union*, 13 April 1993.

50. Steven Sweeney, "Rapp Road Never Meant to Be a Real Through Road," *Albany Times Union*, 8 March 1998.

51. Ibid.

52. Ibid.

53. Danielle Furfaro, "Now on Sale at Mall: Land," *Albany Times Union*, 7 July 2001.

54. Ibid.

55. Fred LeBrun, "The Mall That Ate a Region," *Albany Times Union*, 27 July 1998.

56. Barbara Quint, "Crossgates Expansion Would Affect the Region," *Albany Times Union*, 31 July 1998.

57. Dickson interview, 16 April 2000.

58. Commisso interview.

59. Clabby, "Promised Land That Kept Its Word."

60. Commisso interview.

61. Ibid.

62. Danielle Furfaro, *Albany Times Union.*

63. Ibid.

CHAPTER 5. "I NEEDED TO LET PEOPLE KNOW THE COMMUNITY WAS HERE"

1. Jeffrey C. Stewart and Faith Davis Ruffins, "A Faithful Witness: Afro-American Public History in Historical Perspective, 1828–1984," in *Presenting the Past Essays on History and the Public*, edited by Susan Benson, Stephen Brier, and Roy Rosenzweig (Philadelphia: Temple University, 1986), 334.

2. New York State Office of Parks, Recreation, and Historic Preservation, *Guide to the Survey of Historic Resources Associated with African Americans in New York State* (Albany, NY: State Printing Office, 1997), 1.

3. Ibid., 2.

4. Ibid., 7.

5. Ibid., 14.

6. Ibid.

7. Ibid., appendix III. In 2007, out of the approximately 4,500 designated historic properties in New York State, 92 of these were associated with African American history.

8. Ibid.

9. New York State Office of Parks, Rec., and Historic Pres., *Guide to the Survey of Historic Resources Associated with African Americans in New York State.*

10. Beth Savage and the National Park Service, *African American Historic Places* (New York: The Preservation Press, 1994), 9.

11. Ibid.

12. Ibid.

13. Ibid., 203, 338.

14. Ibid., 345.

15. Ibid., 140.

16. Ibid., 209.

17. Ibid., 293.

18. Emma Dickson, interview by Brian Buff, mini-disk recording, Albany, New York, 16 April 2004.

19. Ibid.

20. Ibid.

21. Ibid.

22. Ibid.

23. Ibid.

24. Ibid.

25. Ibid.

26. Ibid.

27. Ibid.

28. Ibid.

29. Ibid.

30. Ibid.

31. Bonafide interview.

32. United States Department of the Interior National Park Service, *National Register Bulletin #38 Guidelines for Evaluating and Documenting Traditional Cultural Properties* (Washington, D.C.: United States Printing Office, 1991), 11.

33. Ibid.

34. Bonafide interview.

35. Dickson interview, 23 February 2004.

36. Ibid.

37. Bonafide interview.

38. Ibid.

39. Ibid.

40. Ibid.

41. Ibid.

42. Ibid.

43. Ibid.

44. Dickson interview, 23 February 2004.

45. Ibid.

46. Bonafide interview.

47. John Scherer, interview by author, mini-disk recording, Albany, New York, 24 March 2004.

48. Ibid.

49. Ibid.

50. Bonafide interview.

51. Ibid.

52. Ibid.

53. Dickson interview, 23 February 2004.

54. Ibid.

55. Bonafide interview.

56. Dickson interview, 23 February 2004.

Works Cited

INTERVIEWS

Beebee, Patricia. "A Capital Area Oral History," 22 February 1997. Public program recorded on tape. Albany Institute of History and Art, Albany, New York.

Bonafide, John. Interview by author, 24 February 2004, Albany, NY. Mini-disk recording.

Burton, Eddie Johnson. Interview by author, 14 November 2002, Waynesboro, Mississippi. Mini-disk recording.

Burton, Sam. Interview by author, 14 November 2002, Waynesboro, Mississippi. Mini-disk recording.

Commisso, Frank. Interview by author, 2 February 2004, Albany, New York. Mini-disk recording.

Conway, Geneva. "A Capital Area Oral History," 22 February 1997. Public program recorded on tape. Albany Institute of History and Art, Albany, New York.

Dickson, Emma. Interview by author, 19 April 2000, Albany, New York. Tape recording.

———. Interview by author, 16 November 2003, Albany, New York. Mini-disk recording.

———. Interview by author, 23 February 2004, Albany, New York. Mini-disk recording.

———. Interview by Brian Buff, 16 April 2004, Albany, New York. Mini-disk recording.

———. Interview by author, 17 May 2004, Albany, New York. Written notes.

Dukes, Leon. "A Capital Area Oral History," 22 February 1997. Public program recorded on tape. Albany Institute of History and Art, Albany, New York.

Fantroy, Henrietta. Interview by author, 19 April 2000, Albany, New York. Tape recording.

Fantroy, Sammie. Interview by author, 19 April 2000, Albany, New York. Tape recording.

Ferguson, Girlie. Interview by author, 15 April 2000, East Nassau, New York. Tape recording.

Johnson, McKinley. Interview by author, 24 February 2004, Albany, New York. Mini-disk recording.

LaFrank, Kathleen. Interview by author, 24 February 2004, Albany, New York. Mini-disk recording.

McDonald, Alma. Interview by author, 12 November 2002, Shubuta, Mississippi. Mini-disk recording.

McDonald, Dorothy. Interview by author, 12 November 2002, Shubuta, Mississippi. Mini-disk recording.

McDonald, Eddie. Interview by author, 12 November 2002, Shubuta, Mississippi. Mini-disk recording.

McDonald, Willis, Jr. Interview by author, 12 November 2002, Shubuta, Mississippi. Mini-disk recording.

McCann, Nora Lee. "An Evening with Emma," 22 February 2002. Wilborn Temple public program recorded on tape.

McCann, Ralph. Interview by author, 19 April 2000, Albany, New York. Tape recording.

Nabors, Juanita. Interview by author, 17 April 2000, Albany, New York. Tape recording.

Norman, Rhonda. Interview by author, 14 April 2004, Albany, New York. Written responses via email.

Rucker, Orlean. Interview by author, 19 April 2000, Albany, New York. Tape recording.

Scherer, John. Interview by author, 24 March 2004, Albany, New York. Mini-disk recording.

Stamper, James. "A Capital Area Oral History," 22 February 1997. Public program recorded on tape. Albany Institute of History and Art, Albany, New York.

Thomas, Fred. Interview by Emma Dickson and author, 12 November
    2002, Shubuta, Mississippi. Mini-disk recording.

GOVERNMENT DOCUMENTS AND OTHER DATA SOURCES

Albany and Rensselaer, N.Y. Directory. Albany, N.Y.: Sampson and Murdock
    Company, 1920–1960.
National Urban League, Department of Research and Investigation. *The
    Negro Population—Albany, New York*. New York: National Urban
    League, 1928.
Town of Guilderland Zoning Board of Appeals. Meeting minutes 1981.
    Guilderland, New York: Town Hall.
United States Bureau of the Census. *Fifteenth Census of the United States
    Taken in 1930*. Washington, D.C.: United States Government
    Printing Office, 1932.

MANUSCRIPT COLLECTIONS

Haney, Eva and Anna B. Hardee. "Historic Clarke County, Mississippi,
Assignments #10, 19, 26, 57." Washington, D.C.: Federal Writers Project,
    1936.
Mayor Erastus Corning, 2nd, Papers. Albany County Hall of Records.
    Albany, New York.
M. C. Lawton Club Papers. M. E. Grenander Department of Special
    Collections and Archives. University at Albany. Albany, New
    York.
Mississippi Department of Education. *African American Education Folder*.
    Jackson, Mississippi: Mississippi Department of Archives and
    History.
NAACP Albany, New York, Branch. M. E. Grenander Department of
    Special Collections and Archives. University at Albany. Albany,
    New York.
Winchester, Harold. "The Early History of the Albany Inter-Racial
    Council." The Ruth Robert African Americans in Albany Collection.
    Albany Institute of History and Art. Albany, New York.

NEWSPAPERS

Albany Knickerbocker Press. 1920–1960.
Albany Times Union. 1960–2004.
Shubuta Mississippi Messenger. 1914–1917, 1917–1920, 1921–1924.

BOOKS AND ARTICLES

Ballard, Allen. *One More Day's Journey: The Story of a Family and a People.* New York: McGraw-Hill, 1984.

Bethel, Elizabeth. *Promiseland: A Century of Life in a Negro Community.* Philadelphia: Temple University Press, 1981.

Carley, Rachel. *The Visual Dictionary of American Domestic Architecture.* New York: Henry Holt and Company, 1994.

Clarke County Chamber of Commerce, *Historic Clarke County* (Quitman, Mississippi: privately printed, n.d.), 20.

Dansby, Gradie Pearl. *Historic Clarke County.* Quitman, Mississippi: privately printed, 1996.

Davis, Ronald L. F. "Creating Jim Crow: In-Depth Essay." The History of Jim Crow website accessed from http://www.jimcrowhistory. org, 2003.

Du Bois, W. E. B. *The Souls of Black Folks.* Chicago: A. C. McClurg and Company, 1903.

Frazier, E. Franklin. *The Negro Church in America.* New York: Schocken Books, 1964.

Gottlieb, Peter. *Making Their Own Way: Southern Blacks' Migration to Pittsburgh, 1916–30.* Chicago: University of Illinois Press, 1987.

Granat, Diane. "Saving the Rosenwald Schools: Preserving African American History." Alicia Patterson Foundation website accessed at: http://www.alicia patterson.org/APF2004/Granat/Granat.html, 2003.

Grossman, James. *Land of Hope: Chicago, Black Southerners, and the Great Migration.* Chicago: University of Chicago Press, 1989.

Guide to the Survey of Historic Resources Associated with African Americans in New York State. Albany, New York: New York State Office of Parks, Recreation, and Historic Preservation, 1997.

Gutman, Herbert. *The Black Family in Slavery and Freedom, 1750–1925.* New York: Vintage Books, 1976.

Hareven, Tamara. *Family Time and Industrial Time: The Relationship between the Family and Work in a New England Industrial Community.* Cambridge: Cambridge University Press, 1982.

Harris, Clemmie. "Suburban Populism: A Short History on Environmental Politics in the Pine Bush Region from 1950–1982." Master's thesis, University at Albany, 2002.

Jackson, Rose Juan. "The Black Educational Experience in a Northern City: Albany, New York, 1830–1970." PhD diss., Northwestern University, 1976.

Kennedy, William. *O Albany! Improbable City of Political Wizards, Fearless Ethnics, Spectacular Aristocrats, Splendid Nobodies, and Underrated Scoundrels.* New York: The Viking Press, 1983.

Koslow, Philip, ed. *The New York Public Library African American Desk Reference.* New York: Stonesong Press, 1999.

Kusmer, Kenneth. *A Ghetto Takes Shape: Black Cleveland, 1870–1930.* Chicago: University of Illinois Press, 1976.

Lemann, Nicholas. *The Promised Land: The Great Black Migration and How It Changed America.* New York: Vintage Press, 1991.

Marks, Carole. *Farewell—We're Good and Gone: The Great Black Migration.* Indianapolis: Indiana University Press, 1989.

Mason, Jerry D. *Shubuta, Mississippi: Home of the Red Artesian Well.* Shubuta: author, 2001.

McAlestar, Virginia and Lee McAlestar. *A Field Guide to American Houses.* New York: Alfred A. Knopf, 2000.

McEneny, John J. *Albany: Capital City on the Hudson.* Sun Valley, California: American Historical Press, 1998.

Osofsky, Gilbert. *Harlem: The Making of a Ghetto, Negro New York, 1930–1989.* New York: McGraw Hill, 1963.

Ostergren, Robert. *A Community Transplanted: The Trans-Atlantic Experience of a Swedish Immigrant Settlement in the Upper Middle West.* Madison: University of Wisconsin Press, 1988.

Rittner, Don. *Pine Bush: Albany's Last Frontier.* Albany: Pine Bush Historic Preservation Project, 1976.

Savage, Beth and the National Park Service. *African American Historic Places.* New York: Preservation Press, 1994.

Scheiner, Seth M. "The Negro Church and the Northern City." In *Seven on Black: Reflections on the Negro Experience in America*, edited by William Shade and Roy Herrenkohl. Philadelphia: J. B. Lippincott Company, 1969.

Sernett, Milton. *Bound for the Promised Land: African American Religion and the Great Migration*. Durham: Duke University Press, 1997.

Stewart, Jeffrey and Faith Davis Ruffins. "A Faithful Witness: Afro-American Public History in Historical Perspective, 1828–1984." In *Presenting the Past: Essays on History and the Public*, edited by Susan Benson, Stephen Brier, and Roy Rosenzweig. Philadelphia: Temple University Press, 1986.

Trotter, Joe W. *The Great Migration in Historical Perspectives: New Dimensions of Race, Class, and Gender*. Indianapolis: Indiana University Press, 1991.

Washington, Booker T. and W. E. B. Du Bois. *The Negro in the South: His Economic Progress in Relation to His Moral and Religious Development*. Philadelphia: G. W. Jacobs, 1917.

Wharton, Vernon Lane. *The Negro in Mississippi, 1865–1890*. New York: Harper Torchbooks, 1965.

Wilborn Temple 75 Years of Love in the Making, 1927–2002. Albany: Wilborn Temple First Church of God in Christ, 2002.

Index

187